# IMMIGRATED: A MEMOIR

## NADIJA MUJAGIC

PIONEER PUBLISHING

First originally published by Pioneer Publishing 2021
Registered in the Library of Congress

Edited by Elizabeth DeNoma
Cover design by Michael Rehder

ISBN 978-1-7370047-0-7

*This book is a memoir. It reflects the author's present recollections of experiences over time. Some names and characteristics have been changed. Some events have been compressed and some dialogue has been recreated.*

ALSO BY NADIJA MUJAGIC

For a better reading experience of this book, check out the prequel *Ten Thousand Shells and Counting: A Memoir*

*Dedicated to all trauma, war, and domestic abuse survivors.*
*May lightness and peace always be with you.*

*Yet not so much but what I shook with dread*
*at sight of a great Lion that broke upon me*
*raging with hunger, its enormous head*

*held high as if to strike a mortal terror*
*into the very air.*

Divine Comedy, *Dante*

## SPLICED

One Saturday, in early March 1992, my family and I drove back home from our regular visit to grandmothers' in the Old Town Sarajevo. As long as I'd been aware of my own existence, we'd visited my grandmothers every weekend. As always, my older sister Amra and I, teenagers at this time, fidgeted in the back seat of my dad's little yellow Fiat, anticipating our arrival home so we could go and hang out with our friends. On our way home, the city looked more deserted than usual. Things were changing. Yugoslavia was falling apart.

The day after that early Saturday in March of 1992, we celebrated the declaration of the independence of Bosnia, which was no longer to be part of Yugoslavia. The air felt a bit different. Our adult neighbors gathered in small and intimate groups, and speculated whether a war could break out in Bosnia, like the one that was raging in neighboring Croatia. *How could a war start in Bosnia? It is impossible*, most would say. Especially impossible in Sarajevo where people of so many nationalities had lived together in peace for so long.

Amra and I didn't follow any of these events closely, even though we slowly witnessed our Serbian friends up and go to Serbia, or different parts of the globe. The airport across the street from our building was flooded by people who seemed to be fleeing from something as yet unknown. Amra's Serbian boyfriend at the time, Dalibor, broke up with her without any clear explanation as to why, and then left for Serbia. As Amra cried in our room, sharing all the details, we spent the next hours trying to decipher his sudden move. Not until early April did we begin to notice tanks being positioned at the airport and in the neighboring hills. Like naughty children, with no regard for destruction, the Serbs stole the Yugoslav Army artillery and went on to occupy the hills surrounding Sarajevo. They had us in the palm of their hand. And just like that—in a strange quick heartbeat—the war began. Destruction and killing ensued.

The Serbs shelled us relentlessly, tearing our souls and bodies apart. People died every day. Children became orphans. Mothers lost their sons in battle. Women became widows. Hunger. Grief. Despair. Cries during cold nights; screams during frightening days. The Bosnian War raged wild for years to come.

Just down the street from the city hall was the National Library that had been burned down completely at the beginning of the war. The Serbs took advantage of their high-ground position early one August morning, and shelled the library until every single manuscript it contained was destroyed. Those who witnessed the destruction said the ashes flew high up in the air for days until it finally rained. The library remained standing as a reminder of suffering, but also resilience.

EMERGING FROM THE SARAJEVO CITY HALL IN MY FANCY NEW suit, it could have been one of the happiest days of my life. You wouldn't know it from the photographs taken at the time, though.

As you exit the city hall, you are greeted by some buildings shelled to their foundations, some resembling an old block of Swiss cheese—filled with bullet holes. The day I came out of the city hall, the images of destruction were still there. Unavoidable and painful.

I still have a few photographs of that moment; I wore a light olive suit, matching shoes, freshly done curly hairdo with a fancy white pin, and flowers in my hand. A couple of gypsies stood close to the building entrance and begged for change, palms extended. For a second, I convinced myself that the unwanted gypsies had ruined the moment for me.

I had just gotten married. A few months earlier, I had turned nineteen. Gripping the bouquet tightly in my hand, as if someone might steal it, I noticed I was sweating with anxiety, over all the things that had already happened, and those yet to come. At some level, I knew I was too young to be marrying, and I also knew why I'd done it; I'd grown up too quickly. I was only nineteen, but, in my teenage years, I had gained the wisdom and mind of a sage.

The past few years required me to become a music conductor when, in fact, I'd only just picked up a musical instrument. None of us saw the war coming. I was fourteen and had other things on my mind. Having nowhere else to go, my family and I stayed in Sarajevo in 1992 and survived what became one of the longest sieges in modern history. The siege lasted one thousand four hundred and twenty-five days. 1,425 instances of daily horror. In the same amount of time, newborns learn to breathe, bond, suckle, eat, coo, crawl, walk, talk, develop a personality, socialize, play, live, survive...

My sister Amra also married when she was nineteen. She met her future husband in the basement of our aunt's and uncle's building, where we stayed temporarily at the beginning of the war. The basement was the shelter we used to hide from shells and bullets. With the war came the unusual habit of everyone marrying—young and old, widowers and separatees, desperate and lonely. There was a marriage epidemic. When my sister got married, I felt lost and unable to accept that she'd no longer live with us. The house felt empty and lonely without her. Waking up alone in the room she and I once shared, now bred melancholy; mornings were filled with a strange void marking her absence, even though she lived in the adjacent building unit, barely a five-minute walk from our home. Someone asked me at her wedding when I, too, was going to get married. I laughed at the question and brushed it off, saying I wouldn't until I'd at least finished college. I had my priorities straight. I had it all together. But after tying the knot on June 14, 1997, my resolve was proved to be nothing but delusion. I'd succumbed to the trap of marrying, like many others who felt that their bond with another human was the only cure for the past pain.

My new husband stood next to me, holding my other sweaty hand. Calm, he scanned the surroundings catching everybody's eyes and smiling at each person. He stood tall, with brown hair and penetrating deep blue eyes. Matteo had the stature of a confident man. He told me once that on a trip to Spain, people thought he was an actor as he walked down the street—perhaps he was mistaken for a young Tom Selleck—and some approached him to ask for an autograph. He was large compared to Bosnian men who'd become weak as a result of the crushing war, malnourishment and constant smoking. They were living evidence of physical decline caused by hunger, fear, pain. Still, they'd found the Herculean strength to defend their fellow citizens during the war—the long and exhausting war.

When in the company of my parents, Matteo gestured and communicated with his eyes, as he didn't speak any Bosnian, except for the random words that could never advance into a meaningful conversation. Nor did my parents speak a word of English. My mom knew the words "hungry" and "eat" and she'd often pose a question using those words when Matteo came to visit while gesturing by bringing her hand to her mouth. My mother was the kind of person who wanted to please people, her guests, either with food, a smile, or a good story.

I studied English in school, but was by no means fluent. Over time, the grammar made more sense, like math or musical notes, but I couldn't solve a problem or compose a song for the life of me. Perhaps because I was not much of a talker in the first place, I didn't have an urgent desire to develop my language skills. As a result of my lack of mastery of the language, Matteo and I had a lot of misunderstandings and mishaps.

About a year before my wedding, my friend Jasmina and I sat at a table in a bar when a man approached us and asked if he might take a seat. We were at that bar, Jasmina and I, almost every night, indulging in a few beers until our tolerance for alcohol grew. We'd meet a lot of people during our outings, some local and others who traveled through Sarajevo on their long global journey.

Matteo was sitting on a chair between us, and we made a round of introductions. He said he was from Boston. Boston? A city I hadn't heard of before. I questioned whether it was located in the US at all. After we chatted for a while, he turned to me and asked, "How old are you?"

In Bosnia, asking woman's age is deemed inappropriate, so I answered in a most subtle way I could muster.

"Guess," I said.

He looked at me and then raised his eyes to the ceiling, placing his hand on his mouth, pretending to be thinking hard. He gazed back at me, with an amused look on his face, and kept guessing I was in my twenties until he finally said, "Okay, I give up." I told him I was eighteen, and he looked at me, widening his eyes, as if he was surprised to hear how young I really was.

"How old are you?" It was my turn to ask. I didn't care, but I kept the conversation going.

"It's your turn to guess."

I looked at him, the same way he looked at me before he began guessing, and with full confidence, I said, "Forty-two?"

He began to laugh hard and leaned his chair backwards; I thought he was about to fall off. While his head leaned back, I could see all of his upper teeth and his uvula dangling. He was apparently amused by the precision of my guess. Indeed, he was forty-two. Shortly after, that, he stood up and said goodbye, saying he hoped to see us there again. Five minutes later, he walked through the door and came up to me. He whispered something in my ear and then handed me his business card. I had no idea what he said, nor did I care. I put his business card in the back pocket of my blue jeans, and completely forgot about it, until Jasmina reminded me a few days later.

"You should call him." She insisted.

I'd known Jasmina since I was a baby. She lived door next to me in our old neighborhood across from the Butmir International Airport. Jasmina was a free spirit; she liked to socialize, and of the two of us, she was the talker. I'd known her to always make friends easily, and people liked her goofy sense of humor. Unlike for me, small talk seemed to roll off her tongue, and she had story after story to tell, rarely a boring one among them. She talked about any number of subjects that showcased her intelligence and humor, and she'd ask good follow-up questions to keep a conversation flowing. As for me, well, I was the total opposite of that. I preferred to sit there quietly, speaking up on occasion, only when it suited me, and not bothering to engage unless I really had to.

Socializing just didn't come as naturally to me, and so I hesitated to call Matteo. Jasmina convinced me I had nothing to lose; I should call him. One day, I finally mustered up the courage and did it.

When he answered the phone that evening, I was nervous and my palms were sweating when I heard his voice.

"May I speak to Matteo?"

"Speaking. Who's this?" I introduced myself and could sense his happiness immediately. We tried to converse, but his words were like a muffled radio I couldn't quite decipher. I kept saying, "What, what?" and he would either repeat the same sentence or simplify words he had just used. When he asked what I was doing at that moment, I replied, "Nothing. I'm kind of boring," mixing up the adjective with *bored*. He charmingly reassured me that I was not boring, and offered to pick me up that evening in his blue Jeep.

The Jeep belonged to the USAID, a fact clearly spelled out on the side of the car. Matteo had come to Bosnia to work for a Texas-based company under contract from the USAID, to work on reconstructing roads and bridges after the war. Most of the infrastructure had been destroyed, and many companies from different countries were coming to Bosnia for humanitarian purposes. As part of his contract, Matteo was given housing and transportation.

He picked me up that evening and we stopped to get Jasmina. As she lived on the ninth floor, I'd often yell in front of her building, calling her by her nickname *Seka*, which meant *little sister* in Bosnian. I wanted to avoid walking up the nine flights of stairs since neither the elevators nor lights functioned again yet. During the war, we quickly learned to navigate those stairs by counting them and holding our hands in front of us to ensure we wouldn't slam into anything. Over time, as dark nights called for extra caution, our speed improved as our sense of the dark became sharper and clearer.

*Sekoooooo*, I'd call, and my voice would echo along the street. Within seconds, Jasmina would peek through the window and announce she was coming downstairs. Matteo laughed at this form of communication. He was impressed that, of all potential little sisters in the long building, more than ten stories high, only one would know that the call was for her. That night was one of many nights the three of us spent hanging out, drinking, playing pool, or driving around the city or up to the mountains in his Jeep. At first, I thought Matteo was just another cool friend we spent time with. But as time went by, Matteo preferred that he and I go out alone.

On our seventh date, when Matteo offered to pick me up, I decided to introduce him to my parents. When I told them Matteo was coming to pick me up, my mother frantically began to neaten up the house and clean, asking my father to jump in and help. When Matteo showed up at our door, my parents had this strange aura around them; like they'd seen a saint or a super-hero. My mother had the biggest smile; something I hadn't seen in years. Her smiles had been largely exiled during the war, banished by daily tribulations and war losses. There was some-thing about Matteo being an American, at least back then, that was extraordinary to Bosnians. Americans saved us from the Serbs' occupation. They dropped bombs on the Serbian artillery that was sitting on the nearby mountains and hills. They freed us from the three-and a-half year siege of Sarajevo. Americans were reputed to be heroes, and now my mother could experience heroism through Matteo, a person she knew nothing about. But she was okay with that as long as he was verifiably American.

Eventually, and to my surprise, they took him in like a family member. My mother often invited him over for dinner. I didn't tell my parents how old Matteo was, as I suspected they might feel uneasy about the age difference. Surprisingly, they never asked. Matteo looked younger than his age, vibrant and full of energy. People in Bosnia aged much more quickly, unexpectedly, like an overly ripen banana you'd rather discard than eat. Matteo met most of my family members—uncles, aunts, cousins—one day, when my maternal grandmother invited him for lunch. It was the month of Ramadan and my grandmother had prepared a four-course meal. We all sat at the table, and Matteo was the center of attention, questions coming at him from every direc-tion. Matteo smiled and politely answered all of them. My cousin, Edin, still a teenager and happy to be in the presence of an American, drilled him about driving and asked him multiple questions, instantly making Matteo some kind of authority on the subject matter.

"So, is driving the same during day and nighttime?"

"Not quite. You need to be more careful at night, as you can't see that well."

My aunt Šefika didn't speak a word of English, and she waited for her turn to raise a question. At the first opportunity, she shouted as if that would make Matteo better understand the language.

"*Kakva je u vas sofra za Ramazan?*" What's the food like during Ramadan back home in America? She asked this question in all seriousness and we all started to laugh. My aunt Šefika, a good wife to my uncle and a loving mother to my two cousins, didn't have much by way of education. Her ignorance on many things made her the occasional butt of jokes in the family.

The rest of the family could surmise that Matteo was a Catholic. From what I could tell there in the beginning, he didn't care much about his religion. He didn't go to church, he didn't pray, he didn't use the tips of his fingers to make a cross on his head and torso at appropriate times... He never spoke of God. His family came from Italy, so he considered himself an Italian-American. He wore a thick yellow gold chain, long enough so it didn't choke him, but short enough to highlight his neck and make you think of Italian mafia. His initials, M.D., standing for his full name Matteo Damiani, struck him as funny. Once he'd point his finger at himself, laughed and repeated "Doctor, doctor. M.D. Dr. Damiani." My mom took him seriously and told everyone that Matteo was a doctor, as if he'd gotten a PhD. Despite his lack of those educational credentials (he wasn't a doctor of any kind!), Matteo exuded confidence and kindness, so my mom was easily fooled into believing his joke.

My grandmother seated him next to her and kept putting food on his plate. He later told me that the sour cream she had spooned onto his plate was completely covered in mold and looking like a big blue spot sprouting hair. She'd remove the mold from the top and then take another big scoop and dump it onto Matteo's plate. As Matteo told me the story, he laughed so hard, tears fell down his face. I didn't find his anecdote particularly funny, because the war taught me food could be scarce and you could end up hungry and having to eat whatever you could get your hands on—mold or no.

WHEN I MET MATTEO, SUMMER WAS IN FULL BLOOM. TWO
months after we started dating, he asked me to accompany him
on a trip to Istanbul. Turkey was one of the only countries at the
time that allowed Bosnians entry without a visa. Matteo's friend
Leyla lived with her family there, adding another good reason to
visit the country. My mother was hesitant to let me go; she said
no the first time I asked her. I had never been outside of the
former Yugoslavia at that point, so Turkey seemed exotic and
exciting. I wanted to go and see what else was out there. A few
days later, my mother changed her mind, after she had spoken
with her sister who convinced her to let me go.

That summer, Amra got a role as an extra in the movie
*Welcome to Sarajevo*, a movie about the Bosnian war starring
Marisa Tomei, Woody Harrelson, and Stephen Dillane. The real
war had just ended, but someone came up with the idea of
making a movie about it to monetize our suffering and loss.
Amra and her ten-month-old baby girl Dženana packed up and
headed to Split, Croatia, where filming was taking place. Amra
and Dženana ended up only being in one scene in the whole
movie.

The scene went like this:

The chetniks, a Serbian paramilitary group, entered a bus
and began yelling at the passengers. They were armed with guns
and they wore hats with a *kokarda*, the chetnik's symbol of pride.
They screamed from top of their lungs, directing offensive and
insulting words at the women and their children, looking for
someone to hurt or something to damage. They walked up and
down the aisle, searching, prodding, trying to dominate the innocent people in the small space. The scene probably replicated
real experiences during the war. Unlike in real life, though, the
space in the movie was safe. Still, the acting seemed real.

During and after the scene, Amra felt terrified. She was
shaking in fear and felt like real chetniks had come in to rob or

kill them. In the shot, Dženana looked oblivious; she was only ten months old and had no idea what experiences stood behind her mother. She sat on Amra's lap and was bouncing around like a happiest child. By the time they got home, both looked exhausted and pale as if they had been in a real war. As soon as they arrived home, my mother grabbed Dženana, whose little extremities were limp, her body too relaxed for a ten-month-old. My mother cried. After the war, every little thing triggered her sadness.

A nice surprise balanced out the physical toll of the filming. When Amra returned home, she discovered she was paid double the amount she was supposed to be. It was enough to buy a car, but not enough to buy a new car. So, Anis went to a used car dealership one day and settled for an old, half beat up Yugo. It served their needs.

IN NOVEMBER 1996, WITH MY PARENTS' PERMISSION, MATTEO arranged the trip to Istanbul for several days. He bought plane tickets and reserved a room in old town Istanbul. It was my first time ever setting foot on a plane, and I didn't know what to expect. Matteo showed me how to put a seat belt on, and he explained how to move my mouth in order to depressurize my ears while the plane was ascending. He did everything for me— from ordering drinks from a flight attendant, to walking me to the lavatory and showing me how to open the door. We arrived in Istanbul and found our hotel right away. When we unpacked, I noticed that someone had stolen my denim jacket—a favorite gift from Anis, Amra's husband. Matteo noticed that his flannel shirt was missing, too. I figured someone had stolen them from our bags when we went to the lavatory. I was already getting a bitter taste in my mouth about the trip.

When we arrived at the hotel, I wanted to take a shower right away, so I could dress up and be ready to go out for dinner, but when I turned on the water, only cold water came out. A flashback from the war swept over me, as I recalled the days we'd had no running water and had to go down to the basement and fetch it in five-liter canisters, dragging them up the stairs to pour them in a large bucket, and then going back down the stairs again and again. For showers, we'd make a fire on the stove my uncle had procured for us one day, and we'd warm up water hot enough to mix it with cold water and then pour it over our bodies until we finished showering. During the war, lots of people lost their lives in the line for water. This vital substance became the symbol of not only life, but now of death and dying, too. I shivered from the thought of water killing me right there on the spot. This cold water, running innocently through the pipe, became my enemy.

I began to curse in Bosnian, "*U pičku materinu!* Cold water." Matteo had heard those Bosnian swear words many times and knew they came from anger and frustration. He called the hotel receptionist right away to have someone come over and fix the problem. By the time we returned to the hotel that night, the water was fixed, but the night turned out to be more brutal still, because clouds of mosquitos had occupied the room by the time we returned, and we couldn't fall asleep with them flying overhead. As sunlight entered the room early morning, we noticed that a lot of mosquitos had already been smashed against the ugly wallpaper. Matteo decided we needed to find another hotel.

We went to the Four Seasons, a beautiful hotel enclosing a courtyard in the middle. The building had served as a jail in the past and had been converted to a hotel only recently. The luxury of the hotel stunned me, as I had been to only a handful of hotels in my lifetime. When I came into our room, I opened up the snack bar and began eating candy and drinking Coca-Cola. I was hungry for Coca-Cola, for Snicker bars, for foods that I had not seen for nearly four years during the war. It was time to make up for all the things I'd been missing. I had no idea hotels charged much more for these snacks. Each time I grabbed something out of the fridge, Matteo cringed, looking at me as though he wanted to say something, but he contained himself. My innocence prevailed.

During our trip, we toured the city and rented a car that took us to other parts of the country. We went to Bursa and climbed a mountain near the city. Because I was ill prepared, the cold wind blew over me like razor blades and I couldn't stand the elements. We descended into the city decorated with statues of the local and unforgotten hero, Ataturk.

Back in Istanbul, we took a tour of the Bazaar, the Harem, the Blue Mosque, the Hagia Sofia, and we walked around the city. Matteo promised to take me to a mall and buy me a jacket to replace the stolen one.

The mall was a grandiose building like I'd never seen before. The fancy advertisements, flashy lights, mannequins in the windows, high-end clothes displayed. It looked quite different from the sole mall *Sarajka* over which Sarajevo prided itself. During the war, *Sarajka* burned down, becoming a lonely shell sitting in the middle of a city square. When we entered this mall, I felt like I had entered a wonderland, some kind of a strange parallel universe that would eat me alive. I began to feel dizzy and I stopped for a second. I crouched down to the floor, and only then realized that my whole body was shaking, tears falling down my cheeks. I hid my face in my palms in embarrassment, but my whole body was shaking from hyperventilation. I couldn't hide. Matteo didn't know how to cope with my reaction. He stood next to me and let me sob until I calmed down.

Were these tears I'd held back during the war? I didn't know what was happening to me. The crying seemed strange. My perceived toughness and wisdom seemed at odds with my reaction. What had been the trigger? Glamor and beauty? Did the war make me a stranger to these beautiful sights, comfortable with only destruction? I asked that we leave the mall and walk into dark night, where I would feel more comfortable, safer.

A couple of nights later, we went out to a restaurant for

dinner. The fancy restaurant Matteo decided to take me to was near the Bosporus, where fishermen sold their fresh catch for the day. The food was delicious everywhere we went. About half an hour into the dinner, Matteo took my hand and looked me straight in the eye. He was quiet for some time, and then he said:

"Nadija, will you marry me?"

I couldn't believe what I just had heard and asked him to repeat. It wasn't just the matter of English at that point. I was shocked to hear a marriage proposal after only a few months of knowing each other. I didn't know where it had come from, and I didn't think I was prepared for the question. It was the last thing I'd expected on that trip. I simply answered to the best of my ability.

"I don't know. Let me think about it." He agreed and told me to take my time in making a decision.

We spent the rest of the trip touring the city. One evening, we ended up visiting his friend, Leyla, a classmate of his from MIT many years ago. Her house looked huge, the living room decorated with all sorts of trinkets, reminding me of images of the Ottoman Empire. Leyla looked small sitting among her massive furniture. Despite her appearance, her black short hair and small face exuded confidence and largeness. She looked me up and down, examining me, and began asking questions about where I was from, what I was doing back home, how old I was.

When we told her I was from Bosnia, her response, with a touch of sarcasm and spite, was, "Typical Yugoslavian girl." Her voice, the way she said it, still echoes in my mind. She made a face as if I had a bad odor, on top of being Yugoslavian, and then she went on entertaining us with another story.

While I loved the scenery and cultural explorations of the place, the trip left a bitter taste in my mouth. There was too much chaos, and no exit plan. When we checked out at the hotel, Matteo took out his American Express card to settle the bill. It was the first time I'd seen a credit card. I didn't know how credit cards worked, so I assumed Matteo was tricking them and, in a way, wasn't even paying. I thought we had walked away as thieves.

When we returned to Sarajevo, I didn't tell anybody that Matteo had proposed to me. The marriage proposal still seemed surreal. I wanted to keep it a secret in case he changed his mind about it, or in case I somehow had misunderstood the word "marry." In the back of my mind, I kept it as a possibility. Shortly after our trip to Istanbul, Matteo invited me to visit the US. In April of the following year, my dream to someday visit that country reawakened. That trip was to be the beginning of another, entirely new, internal conflict.

# 2

# VISITING THE USA

I always associated springtime with new beginnings and a kind of optimism. In April 1997, I took my first trip to the United States. We stationed ourselves in Boston, but we made a short trip to Denver, Colorado, where Matteo had lived many years ago. His friend, Reggie, a large African American man Matteo used to work with, took us to a steakhouse the first night. Reggie was a single dad and his daughter was in high school. His daughter, excited like a puppy begging for food, wanted to ask questions as soon as we sat at the table.

"We studied Bosnia in school a little. So, *tell me*, what is Bosnia like? I mean, are there any buildings there?"

"Yes, yes, there are buildings there." I retorted. "And we also have cars and stores and restaurants and everything you guys have here." I was annoyed. Reggie looked at me and smiled.

"Oh really? But I don't understand how war can happen in a civilized society. I thought you guys lived in a desert."

I could see her vantage point, the way she looked at Bosnia as a deserted land with savages fighting each other endlessly, like in those old movies where soldiers would face each other on open fields and kill each other relentlessly. How could war happen in the middle of Europe, not far from the cathedrals of Florence or Mozart statutes in Vienna, or the Louvre in Paris? If Europe were a human body, Bosnia would not be anywhere near the heart. It would represent perhaps a small toe or the appendix, parts that were useless, or that the body could function without. During the war, it might have been a large intestine with feces jumbled together, about to explode leaving a mess behind. Europe didn't want to be near the mess. Or clean it up afterwards.

How could I explain all this to her? None of this became clear to me until much later, anyway.

During the trip, wherever we went, the age between Matteo and me was obvious. Not only because he was an already grown man with a rich past behind him, but because the fear in my face revealed my innocence, lack of experience and therefore my fragile, untapped youth.

When we went to shop at stores, clerks would approach me and say: "Can I help you with anything?"

"Just browsing." I picked up those two words from a stranger who I saw get rid of a clerk with those simple words.

"Your father over there..."

I would shoo the clerk away with a quick snap: "He is *not* my father."

Our age difference didn't seem so great in my mind. When Matteo had trouble with his coworkers in Sarajevo, he'd ask for my advice. We'd sit in my room on the floor and I'd philosophize in broken English about life and human relations, and tell him what his best course of action was. He'd listen and absorb. He'd tell me he would follow my advice and smile.

During my visit to the US, I pictured myself living there. Or, perhaps I wanted to run away from the Bosnian ruins and remains of human flesh scattered on the land. America would transform my life for the better. The country seemed so well organized—everything functioned, the roads were in good condition, most people had the means to drive cars, have a roof over their heads, go out, enjoy life. Living in the US seemed appealing.

When we returned to Sarajevo, I resumed my college classes, but I couldn't concentrate on studying. I was in the first year of the pharmacy program. I felt anxious or depressed most of the time. I'd never had an affinity for chemistry, and now I had to study six different types of chemistry. Meanwhile, Matteo's contract with his company was coming to an end, making me grow more uneasy and depressed. I went to him one day and told him I'd finally made up my mind and wanted to marry him.

In the state of mind I was in at the time, I couldn't bear to face the end of the relationship. Or the end of anything. There had been too many tragic endings during the war. Our relationship had been rocky; we'd considered breaking up many times, but we'd always made up. He wasn't sure about it anymore, given the turmoil in our relationship. He didn't want to be with me with the same intensity as he had done back when he proposed to me in Istanbul. He reminded me of our constant fighting, and he raised his concerns about my belligerent reactions. He couldn't or didn't know how to express what they did to him, but he knew he didn't enjoy them.

On one such occasion, I went to visit Matteo in his Sarajevo rental apartment, and he told me that the cleaning lady had unexpectedly quit (or he had fired her?) that day. He needed a new one, so he offered me the job as his personal house cleaner. He thought my family would benefit from the extra income; my parents' salaries were meager and they could barely get by. When he offered me the job, I gaped. My eyes widened in disbelief that he might want to ask his potential future bride to be his servant. Someone he would pay. I told him I'd clean the house for free and stormed out of his house, fuming. I walked home that night. The lamp posts along the main street flickered in the distance, making the path hard to see. As I advanced through the dark night, I resolved to be done with the relationship.

But one day in May, he called me and told me he was leaving

Bosnia at the end of July. His contract was about to expire and he was being sent back home. I began to feel the gravity of the impending separation—another permanent loss I could not handle.

"What about getting married?" I said. Silence ensued. My emotions were a rollercoaster, down again, emphasizing the imparting loss that I could not handle. Matteo, in my mind, had appeared like a beautiful flower in the middle of a minefield, and I wanted to reach out for it, pluck it, and call it mine. The minefield was dangerous. But walking through it to grab the prize might have been worthwhile.

"Yes, yes. Let's get married." Matteo answered.

The following day, Matteo arrived at my parents' house. Whenever we anticipated his arrival, my mother frantically began cleaning the house and ordering my father: "Come on, get ready. Our guest is coming soon."

When he arrived, he was clean shaven, dressed up and smelling of cologne. He sat down next to me on the couch, smiling nervously, and looking at both my parents, readying himself to deliver his lines. He took my hand and began. My parents knew immediately what was happening and they both began to cry, nodding in agreement. It was a done deal. Somehow, I felt cheap and dirty. Did it take this little to become a bride? Nonetheless, it was what I wanted. I got it.

All my friends came to the wedding. The reception took place at my parents' apartment. My mother and our neighbor prepared all the food. We had an accordion player liven up the party. While sitting on the balcony and singing along with a guitar, my sister and I sobbed because we both knew I would soon leave the country and start my life anew in a far-off land. We hugged and sang to the famous former Yugoslav song *Fratello* about a farewell to someone else also going to that distant land, America.

Matteo and I left the party early and went to his place. I didn't want to leave my parents' home. I couldn't accept staying at a place on the other side of the town, not sleeping in my own bed, or waking up to the smell of morning coffee my mom had made. I wanted to stay a bit longer and savor my family's presence, as I knew my time with them was coming to an end. When we arrived at his place, I went to bed, aloof and quiet, turned toward the wall and fell asleep crying.

The following day, we went on our honeymoon, to an island called Brač, in Croatia. While there, Matteo enrolled me in scuba diving lessons. I was having fun learning to scuba dive and exploring the island until one day, in the back of our rental house, I couldn't resist jumping off a ten foot wall. At the bottom was a metal rod I hadn't seen, and I landed on it with all my weight. The blood began to gush and I moaned in pain, unable to move. Matteo rescued me and tried to attend to the wound by rubbing alcohol on it. I was incapacitated for the rest of the trip and could no longer do fun things on the island. To this day, I have a dent on my left shin as a reminder. It looks like someone had moved my skin up with their thumbs, and left it off in the middle of the movement, like they were playing with playdough.

After returning from Brač, we had to make a quick trip to Split, Croatia, to get my green card paperwork squared away. On our way back, we traveled by car through Western Bosnia and passed through towns and cities that had been completely destroyed by the war. The land looked like a Monopoly board an angry person had smashed his fist on, destroying everything. I had been in Sarajevo during the war, where many of the buildings and infrastructure had been flattened to rubble, but the enormity of this destruction looked somewhat surreal. We barely saw anyone on the streets; they looked eerie, like the scariest horror movie.

Our departure to the US was all well planned. Before we left, my father gave me the best advice he could think of at the time.

"Comb your hair often when you get there. Don't let it look messy."

Since the Sarajevo airport was still only minimally functional, we had to take a bus to Zagreb, the Croatian capital, where we would catch a flight to Boston. Amra and Anis gave us a long ride in their Yugo to Tuzla, a city north of Sarajevo, where we would catch the bus to Zagreb. The sadness finally hit me hard, and I felt like my heart was breaking. I sat on a bus seat next to the window and watched my sister wave to me with tears in her eyes.

We arrived in Boston on July 29, 1997. My new life was about to begin. Still, I felt I hadn't had closure with home. My departure seemed too swift, and I wanted to bring pieces of my home with me. But which ones? Too many were broken and I'd had no time to put them together before I said goodbye to the fragmented, beautiful land.

# 3

# ARRIVAL

anding at JFK in New York, we ran through its narrow and dark hallways to catch our flight to Boston. Me shouldering my backpack and an *oklagija*, a three-foot long, skinny wooden pole used to stretch dough for Bosnian pies. It was the only Bosnian item I'd taken, and it represented much about my heritage.

When we arrived in Boston, Matteo's brother, Fabio, waited patiently at the airport to pick us up. He hugged us in welcome, something I would need to get used to in the coming months. In Bosnia, we kissed on the cheek twice to greet someone. The Boston skyline slowly emerged as we exited the airport, showing its tallest buildings, the Prudential Center and John Hancock Tower on the horizon. The Charles River, I later learned, was so filthy it needed to be cleaned in the 1980s and the lyrics "I love that dirty water, Boston, you're my home" by the Standells captured the river's earlier state for posterity in subsequent decades of radio airplay.

As we made our way to Framingham, a city thirty minutes outside of Boston, I became overwhelmed by the flatness of the land, the boring panorama devoid of the kind of hills and mountains that surrounded Sarajevo like beautiful grand green creatures.

That had been my daily view my entire life, a gift to the eye I could not have avoided even if I'd wanted to. We often spent the day in those mountains, looking for forest strawberries, so tiny but delicious, and running through the empty woods. During the war, many battles took place in those woods, and one of my neighbors, Zijo, a toothless, skinny fellow who always wore a smile, died in one. Before he headed to the mountain that day, I'd seen Zijo, told him to take care of himself, and to make sure he returned safely. He smiled at me and said, "Don't you worry. Of course, I will." But Zijo never returned. When I heard of his passing the following day, I didn't cry—my soul had become numb—but, in my head, I thought about people lost during the war. I played back memories of my interactions with Zijo, his sense of humor, and the goodness he so often displayed.

That mountains were now mostly covered in mines, inaccessible by foot after the war. The MINES signs were put up everywhere to avoid them being triggered by careless and heedless passersby. But visually, the mountains remained untouched from a distance. They stood there as my protectors, as a beautiful testament to and a reminder of human resilience.

Here in Boston, there were no reminders of such strength, beauty, and resilience. This land, flat as a pancake, held no meaning for me. I'd have to reform and recreate it, to make it beautiful for myself. I didn't know how far the car was going to take us. We had been driving at least twenty minutes, and I didn't know when our final destination would appear. The Mass Pike highway leading from the airport to Framingham seemed like a straight line, with an occasional curve. The trip was straightforward until we slowed down at a toll booth. It wasn't clear to me why we would suddenly reduce speed and get behind a long line of cars, but soon enough, I saw people handing money to a person in a booth, or dropping quarters in a basket, and then accelerating to full speed and disappearing into the distance.

The ride to our final destination could have taken an hour or four hours—with my distorted sense of time, it was difficult to tell. As I watched the dull scenery of a tree line go by, and had occasional rest stops with gas stations and McDonalds, I navigated my feelings of emptiness.

We arrived at a restaurant and sat at a large round table with Matteo's brother, Fabio, and his wife, Claudia, and their teenage daughter and newborn son. Claudia was a petite woman in her thirties with a beautiful smile and straight teeth, a bit of curly hair framing her face, and her newborn son in her arms. She gave me a big hug and told me she was happy to see me again. Her voice projected certain calm, sounding like leaves rustling in a quiet forest.

When we first entered the restaurant, my steps became unsure. I questioned whether I was doing the right thing by sitting down on a chair I had chosen. When I was growing up, my parents never took my sister and me to a restaurant for formal dining. On rare occasions, they'd take us to Old Town Sarajevo, bustling with fast food diners where you'd buy *ćevapi*, small beef sausages served with fluffy bread *somun*, chopped fresh onion and Kefir. We never needed a table reservation and our visit consisted of a quick in-and-out dining experience. I never learned how to behave in a restaurant: did I wait to be seated? How should I hold a fork and knife? I watched my fellow diners, and placed a napkin on my knees, slowly bringing a glass of water to my mouth and watching the waiters over the rim quickly carry food to their customers.

Right after the war, Jasmina and I met a group of Germans who came to Bosnia to help rebuild the country's infrastructure, and two fine gentlemen decided to take us out to dinner. They took us to a restaurant in downtown Sarajevo, underground. The place had just opened up and had done its best to bring its service up to the before-the-war standards. Instead of appreciating the gesture of being treated to dinner, Jasmina and I giggled together for no apparent reason. The Germans, looking uncomfortable and puzzled, talked among themselves in German, with brows furrowed, most likely making a swift plan to wrap up the evening and exit from our lives forever. We never saw them again. Jasmina and I were still teenagers, war kids, just coming out of the most trying experience, the sands of our lives running through an hourglass before our eyes, leaving only pain and discomfort.

In the Framingham restaurant, fatigue and jet lag began to kick in. I wasn't yet used to the six-hour difference. When the waiter came to our table, I ordered coffee hoping it would perk me up and allow me to carry on with the rest of my day. When a mug of coffee arrived, I looked at it in disbelief that such a watery brown beverage could call itself coffee. I tilted the mug toward me to take a look at the beverage and witness the swiftness with which it sloshed around in the cup, signaling nothing good. I put it close to my lips and sipped it, making a face that said *this can't be called a real coffee.* They all watched, bewildered at my reaction, and Matteo finally said, "Bosnians drink thick coffee in small cups. They take a sugar cube, dunk it in their coffee and take a bite out of it before they take a sip. You should see; it's quite an experience."

"Sugar cubes?" Fabio replied. "We haven't used sugar cubes here in so long."

"Oh yeah, everybody uses sugar cubes in Bosnia. It's interesting to see coffee being a social event where people would just gather and chat for hours drinking their coffee."

"Oh cool. I've seen sugar cubes given to horses," Fabio added. "You can place a couple of cubes on your palm and hand them to Nadija *'here, horsy, here'.*"

Fabio and Matteo began to laugh and the whole restaurant filled with the echo of the vile sound. I clenched my teeth and tried my best to keep tears from forming. Being subject to mockery felt like a knife was stabbing me in the heart. I grabbed my coffee and put the rim to my lips and kept it there for some time pretending to be taking small sips. But I wasn't. I was looking at the patterns of my coffee, the little waves forming at the edges of the mug, and thinking of my family and friends back home, the mountains surrounding my city, and trying to find strength by imagining them sitting with me, in this strange, flat place. The first day of my new life in America was filled with laugher, but I wasn't the one laughing. I closed my eyes, took another sip of my coffee, and asked myself: *is this ridicule only the start of things to come in my future path?*

# 4

# NEW HOME

My new home was a grand Greek revival house, featuring tall columns on the side facing the main street, nine bedrooms, six bathrooms, a large kitchen, and a library. A large back yard lined up alongside one of the busiest streets in Newton, Massachusetts. I never would have dreamt of living in a house like this back in my homeland. A house like this one—half the size of this one—might be found in scattered Bosnian villages, large and grand, made of concrete, and boxy looking, belonging to people who had no luck or intention of living in the bustling main cities. Matteo's grandmother, who was in her nineties, owned the house. She had suffered from cancer and was counting down the days until her last breath. She was short and tiny, reduced in size by the disease. Her hair was thinning from the chemotherapy sessions she had taken over the past months.

She accepted me into her home and grew fond of me right away. We shared a special bond, having had the same experience of arriving in a foreign land at the age of nineteen, alone and lost, finding new identities we could proudly claim as our own. A painting of her as a young woman hung on one of the walls; its image one of a young beauty, with the front portion of her hair covered by a red shawl, the rest of her hair visible behind it, looping earrings, and a look on her face of pride and toughness. Posing for this painting led to her first paycheck after arriving in the US from Italy. Strengthening our bond, I learned she had married a man much older than she'd been, but her marriage did not last and she was bound to raise her two children alone.

Grandmother, as everyone called her, had two daughters, now well in their seventies. Gloria, the eldest, had temporarily moved from Pennsylvania and lived in Grandmother's house taking care of her through her illness. Her other daughter, my mother-in-law, Diane, lived a lonesome and estranged life in a two-bedroom townhouse apartment in Rockport, a small ocean town in the northern part of the state. I saw her only on rare occasions. Her home sat on a large rock that looked like it might collapse any minute. In one corner of her living room stood a piano, an instrument she rarely played. Her home was neat and clean, and her couch was worn from day-in, day-out constant sitting in while she worked on crossword puzzles.

Diane was widowed when the last of her seven children was still in her belly. Her husband, a Harvard graduate, had been the breadwinner. Tall and handsome, no one would've believed he would die suddenly of a heart attack while still in his forties. When the last child, Irene, was born, Diane fell into a deep depression. She seemed to have lost interest in raising and caring for her children. Their big house on Sargent Street, not far from Grandmother's house was sold a few years after her husband's death, and the older children found their way to better lives elsewhere.

When I entered the large Greek revival house, my new home, I didn't realize at first that *my* part of the home would consist of a small room located on the top floor, always too hot in the summer and never quite warm in the winter. Matteo and I shared the floor with a large man in his forties, Joe, whose dark partial beard against his pale skin reminded me of stereotypical Amish. He seemed friendly on the rare occasions we ran into him, when he visited the bathroom across from his room. He often wore only a robe and always seemed to rush back into his room. He almost never left his room except to go to work or to use the bathroom.

I disliked him right away because he showed no interest in cleaning the toilet, and the bathroom was often covered in filth. When we moved in, my first order of business was to clean the toilet, but shortly after each clean, Joe returned it to its usual condition, still uninterested in cleaning it himself, making me hate both him and the bathroom I had no choice but to use. Matteo told me Joe was often busy jerking off in his room, with a pile of dirty magazines lying by his bed, and this information was too much for me to hear, and fueled an even deeper dislike for Joe.

Our room was located at the other end of the hallway; it was tiny and the slated roof on both sides made the room look even smaller. As you entered the room, the bed was on the right, with a large desk directly in front, under the slanted roof. On the left side was a closet, big enough for a few garments I had acquired after the war.

The size of the room made me feel claustrophobic and sad. The nights were unbearable as Matteo snored all night, every night. I'd run out of the room and sleep on the floor in an empty room down the hall, crying my eyes out, missing my mother, my family, and Dženana.

One night before we went to bed, I picked up the phone and called long distance, patiently waiting for my mother to answer the phone. It was eleven o'clock at night, and grasshoppers were chirping outside, signaling a cold fall to come. When my mother picked up the phone, she answered in a somber voice. The telephone had woken her up at five in the morning, and she sounded as if she was lost or drunk or unsure as to who'd be calling that early in the morning.

"Mom, I miss you so much." I could barely speak from the tears. My voice was cracking, my hands shaking from sadness.

The scene reminded me of when I was a small child and my mom had to leave town to visit her sister who had just lost her husband to a heart attack. She lived in a different city so my mother had stayed there overnight. I begged my father to let me call her so that I could hear her voice for even a second. I was only nine then.

Fast-forward ten years and I was that small child again, longing for my mother's warmth, love, and comfort. I so terribly wanted to share the same physical space with her at the same time. I wanted to hug her and stay in her embrace for a while. But I was the one who'd made the choice to leave her behind. In my mind, I thought that leaving destruction, both physical and mental, would cure me, but I did not realize that missing my family and environment, even with its unwanted destruction, was taking its toll. It seemed so much harder to live in this small room, in this big house with its cold walls and darkness.

My mother, still not fully awake, was at first lost for words, but then she told me we would talk soon and that I should stop crying and I was in a better place now. I hung up, running to the other room to sleep there, curled up in a ball, covered with a sleeping bag that Matteo had used on his camping trips in earlier times.

The first few days at our new home were filled with my trying to reconstruct Bosnian life by cooking savory pies and beef stew for the whole family. I already missed the Bosnian food. The food in my new surroundings looked like rubber and tasted bland. I missed my mother's cooking. She was a cook who never failed, not one day of my life, to prepare a meal for all of us. For her, cooking was second nature, and if someone were to hire her to cook in a restaurant, she'd have no problem doing the job.

I used the *oklagija* for the first time and stretched the dough on the large kitchen table, while Grandmother sat and intently watched me stretch the dough, flip it in the air, fill it and place it into a pan. She folded her legs and put her arms on her knees, wearing a bandana to make sure no hair landed on the pie. She observed carefully, taking it in like I was on a cooking show.

But my savory potato and ground beef pie did not come out as I wanted it. The dough was too thick, the ground beef was too bloody, the potatoes were not well cooked. With the failure of making the pie, the Bosnian life I had tried to recreate dissipated slowly.

I began to realize that adjusting to my new life would be a difficult road. This land would be my new home for a long time to come, but it wasn't gelling just yet. I had to get used to all the nuances, the differences in the American people, new customs, language, food. What resonated the most was there were no traces of destruction, and no single building in the city pierced by bullets or shells.

I didn't think I belonged there. The place was nearly perfect. But not perfect enough for me to work through my trauma. Without the reminders of war, I often wondered who I was, and what this new world offered me. Did I need to act differently? Normally? Should I pretend I hadn't lived through a war? I wanted to grab this new world and ride it, like a nice, new bicycle in a park, but I soon realized my path was paved with rocks and mud, and I had to somehow overcome it.

BACK IN BOSNIA, I'D GOTTEN A CAMERA AND WAS INSPIRED TO document all the devastation, like it was something to be proud of, something to show off. I used to wish I had a camera during the war, but they were quite difficult to come by. When the Serbs occupied our home, we lost everything, including a small camera my father had kept in a drawer. After the war, I dreamed of becoming a photographer someday, and before I even had a chance to familiarize myself with my new home, Matteo sent me to a week-long black-and-white photography class in Maine.

Two days after we arrived, I was already on my way to the

class. The trip to Maine seemed long; the roads were wide and beautiful, lined by trees. Were they birches? Or ashes? I could not name them right away. The roads in Bosnia are narrow and windy, and to get from one point of the country to the other, a seemingly short distance could take four to five hours. You'd pray you arrived at your final destination in one piece.

When we arrived, Matteo dropped me off at the campus where people were walking with their cameras hung from their neck, holding onto them like they were their most valuable possessions. I came across pairs of people talking and showing each other their cameras, so enthralled in their conversation that the rest of us did not exist. My first class was to be held on the very same day. We gathered behind a small barn that I later learned was a film developing lab. About ten of us sat on grass, in a circle, which seemed a bit too intimate and cozy-and scary, because if I wanted to escape, I'd be caught doing so. When the time came for people to introduce themselves, I started feeling tension in my heart—my palms were sweating, and my source of air seemed to be disappearing. When others introduced themselves, I paid no attention, instead thinking only of the words I'd utter. What was there to say? *My name is Nadija, and I just came from war-torn Bosnia. I have no experience in photography and my husband sent me here two days after I arrived in the USA. And by the way, I am still jet lagged.*

When my turn came, I mustered up the courage to try to say the most profound thing anyone might ever hear: "My name is Nadija. I am originally from Bosnia. I like the kind of photographs that move soul, that are not just a pose but an incredible action depicted through the camera."

I probably didn't use the words "incredible" and "depicted" because those words would have been too sophisticated for me at the time, but I did mention something about moving souls.

"Moving soul, huh? That is interesting and well said." The instructor replied. I felt relieved that no one was laughing at me, at least not out loud.

In my class was a girl named Patricia, perhaps in her thirties with a flamboyant personality. During the week-long class, I became closest to her as we went strolling down the Maine dirt roads along the coast, looking for new subjects to film. She wore a cap and a shirt hung around her waist, a trendy tank top, a pair of shorts, and winter boots on her feet. Her lively personality contrasted mine, making me shrink to smaller bits and pieces.

During the week we'd shoot, process the film in the dark lab, and develop new photographs, learning different techniques and styles. Back in my room, I learned how to take a selfie with my camera, and I'd stand against the entrance door, put my arms on my head, scooping up my hair, crossing one leg over the other while my stomach was peeking between my pajamas. Then I'd snap photos. When I developed photos, I was pleased with them. In my youth, I looked alluring, staring at the camera boldly, showing off the promise of a wonderful and prosperous future ahead. The instructor and the rest of the class didn't seem moved by my photos. When I came across my portfolio years later, I noticed they looked mediocre at best. I took photos of an old man with a white beard wearing a hat. I came across a lonesome boat sitting on the shore. I found an old graveyard decorated with American flags on almost every tombstone. I had a way to go to make my photography dream a reality.

With all the running around trying to make the most moving art, time quickly passed, and the class came to an end. When Matteo picked me up, we had lunch in a large open space beneath tents protecting us from potential rain. Patricia joined us, and the conversation soon turned lively. In every conversation, I tried to follow and jump in at opportune moments, but talking took place at an incredible speed, with Matteo and Patricia spouting American idioms, fancy words, and jokes I wasn't familiar with.

WHEN WE ARRIVED HOME IN NEWTON, I HOPED TO GET A JOB quickly and begin earning money. My days proved to be slow, often spent visiting Grandmother in her library. I'd catch her sitting in her favorite chair next to the large library desk, staring at a spot on the floor. She had long ago lost her appetite, and her body was resembling a skeleton. I'd often sit next to her on a small ottoman where she'd rest her feet, and I would hold her hands and give her pep talks in my broken English.

On good days, Grandmother would be up and ready to go places, and I'd often tag along with her, going to a local grocery store, Russo's, down the street. She was still driving at the age of ninety, but often she'd stop at a traffic light intended for the opposite lane, and be oblivious to the angry honks other drivers made at her. Once when we entered the store, she cut her finger on something sharp and a blood began to flow. Inside the store, she saw a vase of freshly cut flowers, quickly put her finger inside to wash out the blood and kept on walking with a cane in one hand and a blood-free finger on the other.

At other times, when time was passing slowly and without direction, I'd turn on the computer upstairs and connect to AOL. As I was familiar with neither computers nor the internet, I'd poke around, looking at the images for the desktop icons and clicking on them randomly until something exciting came up. On one occasion, I accidentally accessed Matteo's email and I came across a familiar name, that of the woman I'd recently met in my class, Patricia. I opened the email and saw that Matteo had initiated contact with her, telling her how nice it was to meet her recently and that perhaps they could see each other again. She responded with the same sentiment, neither one even mentioning my name.

In my disbelief and shock, I closed all the windows quickly, as if that would erase the email and my memory. As I felt my body tense, as I entered this unknown territory. I stared at the computer and regretted witnessing this new reality. Had I been dreaming? Had I read it all wrong? Perhaps I'd mistaken Patricia for someone else. And if the reality settled in at all, what was my role in all this? Where did I stand with this new knowledge? I was utterly confused about their newly formed connection. Shortly after, I logged onto AOL again, hoping I had been wrong. But when I opened Matteo's email, the same message was there.

My thoughts ran wild. Reflecting upon their established connection, I could now clearly see Matteo standing next to Patricia, the two of them laughing and exchanging stories about their exciting lives. In my mind, Patricia wore her baseball hat, her disarming smile on her pretty face. The more I thought about her charm, the more it dawned on me that she was better suited for Matteo than I was. Perhaps she could better handle a marriage. Perhaps she could make Matteo happier with her undeniable confidence and joy. Perhaps she had a number of relationships behind her that would better equip her for marriage.

I had underestimated my wisdom and maturity. Next to Patricia, I wondered, what could a nineteen-year-old girl offer to a forty-two-year old man? His age and experience dominated our relationship. I was a little blossom sprouting in the sun, while he was a house plant tucked in a corner. What was I in this marriage, I wondered? Was I anything at all?

# 5

# ASSIMILATION FAIL

Matteo's attempts to better assimilate me began. First, he took me to see Dr. Diamond in West Roxbury, a twenty-minute ride from home, so I could get braces for my teeth. The upper ones looked crooked, and I rarely smiled, in order to conceal them. I looked forward to having my new, straight American teeth. In Bosnia, they would have stayed crooked. Dr. Diamond was an orthodontist aged well into his early eighties. He had been straightening teeth for decades. Every time we visited his office, his secretary, Gretchen, a friendly older lady with bleached hair and glasses, called me 'sweetheart'. On our way to the office in the car, Matteo would play his classical music loudly through his newly installed speakers, dazing all my senses for a second. The pitching voice of the violin disturbed my ears; it sounded worse than fingernails scraping on a chalkboard. At times, he'd enjoy himself whistling to the music, while I hated it. I blocked my ears and told myself it would soon pass, but neither the violin nor the whistling disappeared fast enough.

Sometimes, when he didn't play loud music, he told me stories about how many women he had slept with. He told me a story about a woman in Borneo who had insisted she perform all kinds of acts on him. He expressed his annoyance as he continued to share he didn't like that, because he wanted to go down on her and enjoy himself.

With stories like this, my jealousy grew and mixed with a growing sense of inadequacy and confusion. I could never match his experience. As he bragged about his love affairs, I shrank into nothingness, and all I did was listen, trying to fend off my feelings of smallness. There was no help from the outside.

Riding in the car with Matteo, wherever we were going, became unbearable. I'd feel tense, as if my body was about to launch into space with my head serving as a spear. One time, when I headed downtown to the Boston Public Library, I asked him to drop me off at the bus stop. By then, I had learned one single bus route and was comfortable taking it alone. But that particular morning, he refused to give me a ride because, for some reason, it didn't seem convenient. At other times, I'd miss a ride, as he'd leave the house early because he had to prepare for a meeting at work, or finish a project that had been lingering for days.

One evening, while we were sitting in the kitchen, our new housemate, a student at Boston College, walked into the kitchen to grab something from the small space of the fridge belonging to her. She had long brown hair, and she was so confident it seemed like she owned the place when she walked in. And then she said, "Matteo, thank you so much for giving me a ride this morning."

I quickly turned my head to look at Matteo and noticed slight discomfort, as if he'd just been caught in his deepest secret.

"You're very welcome," he nearly whispered.

Enraged, I walked out of the kitchen and locked myself in my room.

Who was Matteo? He was transforming day by day, like fire

to ash. The next occasion he drove me to see Dr. Diamond, he switched his music choice from classical to rap, blasting Nelly's songs to show off the new speakers in his leased Toyota 4Runner. I sat next to him, stunned, and wondered how this could have happened. It was like getting a ride from a grandfather one day, and a teenager the next. He had a persona that changed colors like the seasons of the year, like a the texture of a scab on a wound.

On his good days, he'd try to help me adapt and feel at home. He'd found a Bosnian couple, students at MIT, who invited us to visit their dorm apartment near MIT. It was a Saturday evening, sometime after dinner, when we headed over to see the couple. We arrived at their small apartment, and when they opened the door to greet us, they spoke in English. They were married, but they looked like a brother and sister, both wearing glasses with the same looking smile. They couldn't have been much younger or older than me, but they seemed to be taken by Matteo's presence—an alum of MIT who might impart some unknown wisdom to them. They barely had Bosnian accents, and they seemed to prefer to speak only English. While speaking, they stared at Matteo the whole time. There was no exchange between us: they didn't ask me who I was, what I was, where I came from, what my war experience was like. Nothing. I was tongue-tied and I didn't know what to say in the absence of the kind of typical Bosnian conversation that would have naturally taken place after the war. I felt like a piece of furniture that had been brought in and would be placed or discarded as a poor fit later on.

When *Saturday Night Live* came on, they bragged about how they watched it religiously every weekend, and how funny it was to them; it reminded them of a similar show *Top Lista Nadrealista*, a popular show in the former Yugoslavia. I knew the show well. It portrayed the pre-war situation in the country comically, with the well-known Bosnian sense of humor, and like SNL, we watched it religiously and repeated the lines in school for days to come. I thought this would have been a good chance for the three of us to connect, to reminisce about some of the stories or lines from the show, but none of us took the opportunity.

I couldn't, because I was not there.

When we left, to my surprise, Matteo expressed his disappointment in meeting the couple. "I am so sorry," he said. "I don't think I want to see these people again."

I agreed.

Sometimes, we went to parties with his American family and friends, and I found myself roaming around, looking for alcohol to drink to calm my anxiety before I struck up a conversation with anyone looking remotely friendly. I'd start talking about Bosnia, how much I missed my family and friends, and the war experiences that I'd left behind. Most people would excuse themselves after a short time with the familiar line "I am going to get another drink," and I'd never cross their path again. Each time I was shunned, I'd shrink smaller and try to make myself disappear, to become invisible.

One time, when we went to a Christmas party, a family friend came up to me, and began asking questions. I went to my old spiel, careful not to reveal too much information so I didn't scare him away or offend him. When he heard some of my stories, he said, "You know what? You need lots and lots of love, that's what you need," and then he flew away, as if he was some kind of an angel with an important message to impart.

But when Matteo showed up to check up on me, he immediately shared his opinion. "That guy is a dick. Don't listen to anything he has to say."

Matteo later revealed that, years ago, this person had seemingly tricked his mother into selling her home on Sargent Street for less than it was worth, and ever since, Matteo had hated his manipulative guts.

But did the sudden angel know something I didn't? Could he sense my pain, my inadequacy, or my sinking self-esteem?

I was utterly lost in this foreign land of opportunities. Trying to dig my way out of this hole and find myself was a task I didn't know how to begin.

If someone told me today that I was bipolar back then, I'd probably agree. At times, I laughed at beauty, at things that sounded funny, but a few moments later, tears would flow down my cheeks. Sadness arrived every time I thought of my family and my niece growing up without my love and daily affection enveloping the beautiful fragile flower that she was. I missed kissing her plump cheeks and carrying her places in my warm and tight embrace. Before I left for the US, she had just turned two, and was beginning to talk. At times of sadness, I'd call my sister-in-law Claudia's house, and start crying without saying a word. Claudia would realize immediately it was me on the other end of the line.

"Nadija, I'll come and pick you up. I'm leaving my house in fifteen minutes." She'd arrive at Grandmother's with her baby son, say hello to my housemates, and take me to her home in Framingham to comfort me.

I WAS ENTHUSIASTIC ABOUT THE POSSIBILITY OF FINDING A JOB. I decided it would be a distraction from feeling lonely and lost in the new, unknown territory. I grabbed the newspaper one morning and pored over the ads section to see what job I could find. The economy was booming back then, and despite the high interest rates, everyone had prospects and a chance to win.

I read an ad about a job that seemed especially appealing because it required little to no experience. The company was looking for a responsible, honest, and tidy person—it described me, perfectly! I picked up the phone and in my broken English said:

"Hello, I read your ad in newspaper, and would like to apply for the job."

The woman on the other side of the line was friendly, so

friendly I thought she might have offered me the job right then and there.

"Excellent!" She replied. "We would like to meet all the candidates in person, so I am wondering when would be the best time for you to come to our office."

With no plans during the day and nothing to do, I suggested, "How about tomorrow?"

"Perfect!" She responded. She gave me the address, which I asked her to repeat several times until I finally jotted it down correctly. She thanked me profusely and hung up the phone. I sighed and smiled, feeling a sense of relief and a hint of success.

Back at home, I would still have been a student struggling with chemistry and other subjects. When I first enrolled in the pharmacy college, I'd go to the lectures every day and then lab sessions where we'd mix chemicals and tried to pass mini exams. Over-ridden by depression and anxiety, not only did I not understand the subject matter at hand, but I had a hard time speaking up in lectures and sessions and often delayed taking exams until I was feeling better, and more confident.

On my way to a lecture one day, I stopped by a kiosk where hamburgers were sold; I didn't want to go to the lecture hungry. When I ordered a hamburger, I was surprised at what came out of my mouth while my eyes were squinting, seemingly forcing the words: "Ham, ham, ham haaaamburger, please." The "ham ham" part sounded like it had come from a funny sketch—the laugh line in a new cartoon that everyone would repeat and make fun of for days to come.

I was happy to escape that unbearable situation.

Relieved to have a job interview the following day, I decided to take the English-Bosnian dictionary in order to better learn what type of job I had just applied for. I skimmed through the pages of a small dictionary to get to the J section, and finally found the word I was looking for: *Janitor*. I read the definition: *a person employed as a caretaker of a building; a custodian.*

The words took me back to the time Matteo had asked me

to be his house keeper for his apartment in Sarajevo. In an instant, I felt my stomach tightening. I tried to push the memory away as though it were a terminal illness eating my body and soul. I resolved not to show up for the interview the following day.

Coincidently, that same day, Matteo came home and announced he'd found an internship opportunity for me in South Boston. Eager to pursue my dreams of becoming a photographer someday, I embraced the possibility of meeting famous photographers and learning from them. However, the place was not a photographer's studio, or a class, or anything remotely related to learning about photography. It was a photo stock agency where photographers submitted their photos for paid use by newspapers and magazines. The stock agency had photos with subjects ranging from a girl holding flowers to butterflies in the air.

The photo stock agency was next to the ocean on Dry Dock Avenue, a long tall, dull and boxy shaped building, which looked like it might have been recently transplanted from East Germany.

On the first day, I showed up with Matteo so he could introduce me to the owner, Pam, and the office manager, a younger man named David. They enthusiastically expressed how happy they were for me to start. Pam was a on the short side, skinny with dyed blond hair, full of energy and with a loud and confident laugh. David, on the other hand, was a man of Latin descent, always spoke calmly, and often smiled showing off his perfectly white, straight teeth on his goatee-beard face. Without a doubt, Pam was the boss.

The job started immediately, I'd make my way by bus downtown, then take a shuttle to Dry Dock Avenue. At first, I was confused by Boston's public transportation. What do buses even look like? Where do I catch one? How do I pay for it? Where does it drop me off? Would I miss my stop? I felt like Alice entering Wonderland. But with each day, I got used to my routine, catching bus 501 to the South Station, then the shuttle that waited on a street alongside the South Station T stop. If I kept to the same routine, I wouldn't get lost. When I first arrived in Boston, I was told: if you ever get on the metro (or as Bostonians call it, the T) avoid the orange and blue lines. No need to get on those. The colors quickly became my friends in trying to orient myself.

Matteo occasionally took me on road trips and on seemingly endless rides to go sightseeing in different parts of the city. We'd go downtown and when we came close to the Prudential Center, he explained there was a tower on the top that changed colors depending on the weather:

*Steady blue, clear view*
*Flashing blue, clouds due*
*Steady red, storms ahead*
*Flashing red, snow instead.*

MY DAYS AT THE PHOTO STOCK AGENCY SEEMED LIKE *JAJE jajetu* or "egg to egg"—always the same, without anything I could learn, or the excitement of meeting a famous photographer. The studio space was large, about three-thousand square feet, with high ceilings and windows so tall they covered almost the entire height of the wall. Every day, we took orders from magazines or newspapers for a particular image, and then Pam and I would look through the database and search for those images. We used a magnifying glass and would land it on the positives to see if the image resembled one of the orders. Once we'd located the perfect image, we would package it and send it to the magazines.

On the second floor was a photography store, selling all kinds of cameras, film, and photography equipment, and more often than not, Pam and David would send me downstairs to get discounted film to replenish our inventory. When I arrived one day, a couple of young fellows stood behind the counter, and when one of them saw me, he said, "What can I do for you... intern?"

They looked at each other and both began to laugh. I spat out the words I had memorized for the product I had to buy, paid for the merchandise and quickly walked away with tears in my eyes.

When David saw me distressed, he asked me what had happened, and when I told him, he proceeded to tell me that some people can be mean, but that I shouldn't take it personally. He added that there was no shame in being a beginner pursuing a dream of becoming a photographer. His kind words resonated, and instead of feeling sadness, I suddenly felt anger at how those men had attempted to humiliate and hurt me. To make me feel better, David decided to buy me lunch that day. He said, "I buy, you fly," giving me a twenty-dollar bill for two sandwiches. At the end of the building stood Au Bon Pain on the ground floor, one of the few places we could buy lunch.

With David's kindness, I felt safe there. I worked hard and would do anything Pam or David asked me to do. At times, they had me hang all the heavy studio backdrops up on the wall, the ones recently returned by our clients. Skinny and weak, I struggled to prop it up, and would slowly run it against the wall until it was safe on the hook. I'd pause and wait to regain my strength and then hang another one, then another one.

When I realized my hard work wasn't going to compensate me either monetarily, or by teaching me valuable skills, I decided to walk downtown and find a paying job. One day, I told Pam and David I was going to take a walk, and I took the shuttle bus that dropped me off at the South Station. I crossed the main road and found myself in the midst of city bustle with people walking fast, barely paying attention to each other, and brushing up against each other's shoulders. On one corner of a building stood Macy's, with multiple entrances and windows along the entire street block.

I can't recall how I came across the job, but one of the beauty companies, Estee Lauder, was running a two-week promotion, and was looking for an extra cashier. I approached the small kiosk and inquired about the job. I filled out an application and was told I would hear their decision soon. They'd pay me minimum wage and the job would only be available through the promotion. I happily agreed.

The following day, I heard from them and they told me I was hired and should show up the following Monday. Happy I would be earning a salary at last, I went home and announced the news to Matteo, expecting the same kind of enthusiasm for my successful employment. But instead, he burst into flames and began to shout.

"You stupid, ignorant bitch! How could you do this without talking to me first? You stupid, stupid bitch!"

I was taken aback. *Wait, I am a stupid bitch?* How could this be? How could my husband call me mean names like this? Where did it come from?

I went to my room, closed the door behind me, and began to cry uncontrollably. I consoled myself, thinking that maybe Matteo had made a big mistake calling me names, even though his words deeply pierced my heart.

When I came to my senses the following day, I resolved to stick with my decision and to announce my last day at the stock agency to Pam and David. They seemed sad to lose a helper like me, reliable and honest—a hard worker always showing up on time and, of course, doing everything for free. The only thing either of them had ever given me, apart from lunch that one time, was a bottle of apple cider one Christmas. I'd taken pictures of it against the colorful gift-wrap background and mailed the photos to my parents. The photos came out awkward, the bottle out of focus, but I felt proud of what I had earned.

The following Monday, I showed up at Macy's ready to operate the cash register. The manager of the Estee Lauder kiosk was a young woman who always had a few layers of makeup on—pretty, but silly and mindless. One of the sales girls, Aida, was Bosnian and had come from Sarajevo at the onset of the war with her mother and brother, Adnan. Aida wasn't much older than me, but we had nothing in common, and I didn't feel particularly close to her. She flirted with her customers, like a true sales person, and she would show up at work in a blue mini dress that served as her work uniform, with mascara exaggerating her big brown eyes and a thick layer of red lipstick that shaped her lips like a heart. I soon found out her brother had been a classmate who'd bullied me in middle school. How they'd ended up in Boston did not interest me at all, so I didn't even ask. She and I would occasionally exchange a few words in Bosnian, and when the manager heard us speak in foreign tongue, she'd turn around and, as if she were performing on stage, say, "Speak English!" and start laughing.

But there weren't too many opportunities to chat. The Estee Lauder kiosk was surrounded by vultures, women circling around, poking and prodding different products, checking out the displayed perfumes, and dying to get a hold of that free gift, a tote with extra makeup in it, with their minimum purchase of twenty dollars. I had never seen such commotion and chaos over makeup, as I busily rang the register to record all the sales.

As my two-week trial period came to an end, I was again at a loss as to what to do. I liked earning money and was proud of my first paycheck, but what I wondered what I'd do once this job was over. Someone told me the men's knits department at Macy's needed a salesperson and I should apply there. So I did. I soon got word back that I'd gotten the job and should easily transition to it from the makeup kiosk, given it was just another part of Macy's. In the men's knits department, I was responsible for working the register and folding the clothes after careless customers left a mess behind.

One day, the manager sent me to work in the muffin section

as they were short-staffed. I stood behind the counter and waited for customers to approach and order muffins. I'd carefully put them in a bag, or box them, depending on how many a person ordered, and then ring in the purchase. An older lady came by and ordered a dozen muffins. Never hearing the word "dozen" before, I exclaimed, "A *thousand*! I am sorry, but we don't have that many muffins."

The lady looked at me coldly, and repeated, "I said *dozen*. A dozen is twelve."

I was relieved to go back to the men's knits department soon after because I was almost sure that no one would ever ask for a dozen shirts or a dozen pants or a dozen sweatpants. In the meantime, the manager had hired a tall man around my age, Dan, whose dream was to move to Hollywood and become a famous comedian. He was a redhead with freckles, and on slow days, he'd impersonate our colleagues and our manager, and I'd laugh and laugh.

After work one day, we got a six-pack and hid in a nearby park and drank, like naughty teenagers would, talking about our unfulfilled dreams and laughing at anecdotes from Macy's. When I returned home that night and told Matteo what I had been up to, he began yelling and screaming. He called me a stupid ignorant bitch again. He pushed me against the wall in front of our room. He put his index finger up to my face, screaming things at me. I couldn't absorb or remember what things exactly. He yelled loudly and nothing else mattered at that moment. Nothing else seemed relevant. There was silence inside me, a numbness that I'd acquired from the war and its aftermath. That numbness let me think that everything was all right, even when it really seemed to be crumbling to pieces, with no way to get out, with no one to help.

I realized then and there I was not a new bride Matteo was proud of, but I couldn't say anything to my parents because I didn't want them to worry about me. I didn't want to admit to myself or others that I'd made a terrible mistake by marrying a man who, day by day, was slowly becoming a monster and from whose claws I couldn't easily get out. Where would I go? I had no family or friends to help me. Who could I talk to? I didn't know anyone, and the person I felt closest to at the time was a goofy guy at Macy's who was prone to getting me into trouble.

I sank deeper into my own insecurity, realizing I was crossing into a space of not belonging anywhere, not in the USA nor Bosnia. I was becoming a smudge on a map, attempting to survive this new cruelty. I'd close myself in my room (one that Matteo was suddenly paying Grandmother to occupy) and daydream about some reality that was happier and more peaceful than the one I lived in.

ONE DAY, MATTEO CAME HOME AND CHEERFULLY SAID, "I bought something for you. Guess what?"

"I have no idea." It could have been anything. Deep down, I was hoping it'd be a one-way plane ticket to Bosnia.

"I bought a noise machine for my snoring." He laughed. I'd rather he'd bought me a plane ticket.

I longed to be with my parents as if I were a child, needing affection, and reassurance that the world I was about to enter would be friendly. My parents, when my sister and I were growing up, showed their affection differently—Mom was loving, and Dad aloof—but Amra and I both knew our parents wanted the best for us, instilling good values. My mother seemed protective when our father played rough with us. One of us would end up crying by the end of the play session. My father was unaware of his own physical strength and what it did to little children. He once grabbed my cousin by the arms and spun him around and around until a bone in my cousin's little arm cracked.

I will never forget the cold winter days when my parents

bundled me up and drove me in my father's little yellow Fiat to the hospital every morning for a whole week when I was sick. I was about eight years old, and by then I was used to getting sinus, throat, and ear infections all the time. The trips to the hospital could have been avoided had I not had a fear of swallowing pills. When I got sick with a nasty cold, the doctor would prescribe oral medications, and I'd try and try swallowing the pills, to no avail. I outright refused to take them one day; it seemed like a real struggle and I didn't want anything to do with them. My mom attempted to trick me one time by putting a pill in my food, hoping I wouldn't notice it and would unknowingly and magically just take it. But like a little detective, I'd find it immediately, like I had pill sensors, and remove it from my food. My mother didn't yell or give me a hard time or say anything. She made a deal with my father to take me to the hospital first thing in the morning so I could get a vaccine instead. They woke me up gently and got me ready for the hospital trip, a ten-minute car ride from home. They drove me back home and then headed to work, bright and early. I might have not seen it back then, but that was pure love, the kind of love I would never feel from anyone else again.

I was extremely attached to my mother when I was growing up and often sought her company in the middle of the night, getting up from my bed and going to her room to sleep next to her. With my parents' love and affection, I was a free spirit, even teaching myself to read and write at the age of five. My sister would come from school—she was in the first grade while I was still waiting my turn—and I'd get her backpack and take all the books out to see what she had learned that day. I would go over the ABC book and memorize the shape of each letter, teaching myself to pronounce and stitch them together until they were flowing as easily as the words out of my mouth. At age six, I began to write poems. My uncle Keko's best friend Kemo would visit and ask me to share my poems, and I'd take my notebook out of the drawer and give it to him. He'd read poems one by one, and amusingly laugh out loud as if he'd just heard the best joke in the world.

While poetry was my forte at the time, I also enjoyed writing short stories.

I wrote my first story about a young girl who went on vacation to the Adriatic Sea. On her first day, she walked to a table where locals were selling cheap jewelry and trinkets to tourists. The girl ended up buying a silver ring. However, on that same day, she went swimming and when she came out of the sea, she noticed her ring was missing. The conclusion of this devastating story was the childish twist: *how could she have lost her ring the same day she bought it?*

Another story was called *March 8*, which was about the International Women's Day we celebrated in the former Yugoslavia by buying flowers for the women we loved and respected in our lives. The story revolved around me as the main character buying my mother flowers *and* lipstick. As a child, I could only daydream of such a purchase, because Amra and I typically did not have any extra money lying around. My parents would leave us money for bread and whatever else we wanted to have for breakfast (my obvious choice was always Nutella) and we'd buy fewer items on March 8 so we could afford to buy a March 8 gift for our mom. We ended up buying her a single bubble gum, Bazooka, and a small bag of *Smoki*, a puffed corn-meal snack, wrapped up with paper from our school notebook. In my story was a sentence that went like, *Trčala je ulicom i sve je to željela*, or in translation, *She ran on the street, and wished for all of that*, which even in the original language, Serbo-Croatian back then, did not make any sense.

My stories failed to gain any type of recognition or fame, but I kept writing.

In first grade, I got my first publishing gig when the teacher asked that we write a poem or a short story in our Serbo-Croatian class. I wrote a poem about a stuck train, based on the book

*Vlak u snijegu*, or *Train in the snow*, a children's novel by a Yugoslav author, Mato Lovrak. I wrote it in no time and submitted it to the teacher. The next class, I learned my poem was so good my teacher fixed only a couple of words here and there, and then submitted my poem for the school magazine *Elan*. The poem rhymed and had a hilarious twist.

Was I funny as a small child?

My family, both nuclear and extended, thought so. My mother often recalled anecdotes from when I was a kid, and would tell one in which my father went to the back of our building to beat our living room rug. Back then, beating carpets and rugs with a metal stick was the best cleaning method. We'd throw the rug to him from our second-floor window so he didn't have to carry it. When he was done beating the living daylight out of the carpet, making it dust-free, my small head would peak through the window and yell out, "Why don't you throw it back to us now?"

My father once started a house chore and, surprised he'd taken the initiative, because chores were a foreign concept for men in Bosnia back then, I teased my dad, "Did you decide to do this on your own, or did Mom make you do it?" My parents quoted that line for many years.

Another time, my mother's aunt came to visit us, and while her husband, my mother's uncle, was parking a car, Auntie was already sitting on our couch, exchanging niceties, wondering how we had been. When I noticed she wasn't taking anything out of her purse in the form of a gift for kids, as was custom in Bosnia, I finally said, "Thank you, Auntie, for not bringing us anything. That's great."

"Oh, don't worry. Uncle is bringing it with him. We left it in the car." My mother laughed, and I felt relieved.

I repeated these stories in my head, often reminding myself of how it felt to be accepted and loved. I was hoping my new, terrible world would be somehow erased, like sand covered by a wave, where you'd never see the same specks again. As I reflected on these stories, I longed for my family even more, and wished the spirit of love would waft in the air again, like the delightful smell of an apple pie baking on Christmas Eve.

But I suddenly realized the brutal truth—that I was not a new bride to be proud of. Instead, I was a new burden.

## ❧ 6 ❧

# CHILLING DISCOVERIES

Back in Sarajevo, when Matteo and I were getting to know each other better, he divulged his deepest secrets to me. That he had a sudden urge to unburden himself of his shame was evident when, one night, we were sitting on the floor of my room and he told me he had something serious to discuss. He thought it was important for him to tell me certain things about his life if we were going to be a married couple.

I tensed, not sure what was about to unfold in front of my eyes. On one occasion, I asked him if he'd ever been jailed. He answered no. I asked him if he'd used heavy drugs, he said no. I asked him if he'd ever murdered a person, and he just looked at me as if I had lost my mind. So, what could it be?

He sat on the floor, his elbow on the couch, and before he rested his head on his hand, he adjusted his Rolex on his wrist by giving it a gentle shake. He took a pause, looking at a spot in a distance, before he began to share his story.

"I was molested when I was a child." His voice sounded grave and serious. It made me shiver.

"Molested?" That sounded like some kind of food—molasses perhaps—something you'd lick from your finger and it would be tasty. But I doubted that was it. "Molested? What does *molested* mean?"

"When I was six years old, my uncle Sam would come to my room and tell me to take off my pants and underwear." My eyes widened, but I didn't say anything. After experiencing the war, everything seemed less shocking to my ears. "He would then... you know, perform on me. And it felt good at first. I didn't resist at all, and I didn't tell him to stop."

"Did you tell anyone at the time?"

"No. I didn't."

"Why not?"

"I don't know. I didn't think it was wrong at the time. He made me believe what he was doing was a good thing. He'd ask me at the end of his visit to keep it a secret between us."

Keeping a secret of shame was something I knew and had done, so I understood him. When my classmates bullied me at school every day, I kept it a secret from everyone, including my family and Jasmina. Shame had a way of keeping you quiet.

"How long did this go on?"

"Until I was about twelve years old. When I started dating and had my first girlfriend, I finally told him he had to stop. When he tried it, I was resistant and finally told him to leave me alone. And he did."

Uncle Sam was now an older married man who had instantly became my adversary. I had no interest in meeting him, nor did I have the chance to, since Matteo cut off contact with him ever since he realized his uncle's act was a crime. Many years later, when Uncle Sam died, Matteo spilled out his secret to the rest of the family: his sisters, his brothers, mother, all his aunts and uncles, Sam's siblings, and they all denied it vehemently. They told Matteo it couldn't be true— that Matteo was lying. Sam would never do that. He was a good father and uncle, and they could attest to his other good deeds, as well.

But Matteo didn't have to say anything to prove the truth. In my eyes, he was damaged goods, a fact that was slowly being revealed through the first months living in my new home.

I learned bits and pieces about his life before I moved to the United States. He told me he'd traveled around the world, finding jobs in all corners of the globe. He spent time in the South Pole, working at McMurdo Station—a photo of him sitting at the point of the south pole eating pasta in his tank top and mustache while everything looked frozen, still hung on the wall. He'd lived in Asia, in France, taking jobs in the most exotic places to escape home and reality of it. His family once thought Matteo might be a spy working for the CIA, but it was bold speculation, hard to prove. During those numerous trips, he slept with hundreds of women, and he prided himself on knowing how women all over the world were shaped differently, their vaginas either deep or shallow, their breasts small or large, butts flat or plump. He told me once I had a classical body, and he certainly had plenty to compare me to.

Eventually, I learned Matteo's quirky little habits. When we went to a restaurant, he'd turn around to customers on the next table, point his finger at a plate with leftovers and say, "Are you gonna finish that?"

The customer would pause for a second, either confused or bemused, and then reluctantly push the plate toward Matteo.

"Um, yeah, go ahead if you don't mind my germs." Matteo would grab their plate and put the remaining food in his mouth and chew like he'd just won the lottery.

This Matteo seemed different from the one I first met. Back in Bosnia, he had gentleman-like manners, opening doors, smiling politely, tipping well, and never asking for someone else's germs.

Other times, when we visited his brother Fabio, he'd sit at the dining table, put his finger in his nose, and pull a huge booger out, showing it to all of us before placing it in his mouth. He'd start laughing, amused at his own provocation. We all reacted in disgust, shaking our head and telling him to just stop fucking doing that. At home, he clipped his nails at his desk and instead of discarding them in the toilet or trash, he pushed them over the edge and left them slowly piling up on the floor behind his desk.

I was completely disgusted and angered.

Matteo liked to instruct me about all sorts of topics in our conversations, even preaching as to why a toilet paper roll should be used his way, as opposed to another way. He was in no way shy about offering his opinions.

Once, when we were sitting in a restaurant by the Charles River, next to an older couple looking out to the river, deep into a conversation, I turned to Matteo and said, "I bet these two people have traveled all over the world."

"Want me to ask?"

"Sure, go ahead."

Matteo stood up from his chair and approached the couple. I could hear them talk given our proximity.

"Hi, I'm sorry to interrupt your lunch here, but my wife and I were talking, and she made an observation that you might be well traveled and have visited a lot of countries." The man wasn't fazed at all and he seemed amused.

"Sure, you can say that," he responded. Matteo began to talk about his own travel adventures, and then he stopped suddenly, and exclaimed, "Wait a second. You're Howard Zinn. You gave a lecture when I was a student at MIT."

"That's right. I did, a few years back."

"How wonderful to meet you." Then he pointed at me. "My wife here is from Bosnia originally. She lived through the most recent war."

"I am so sorry," he said. "That war seemed quite complex and devastating."

Why was Matteo telling this unknown man about my war history? I learned only later that Howard Zinn was a famous historian. Before we said our goodbyes and departed, Howard gave us his email address. Matteo talked me into writing to him and sharing some of the war stories I had written for my ESL class, which I did. Howard emailed me back a couple of days later to thank me for sharing, and that was the end of our exchange.

Matteo's lack of shyness only deepened my feelings of insecurity. I'd often sit quietly when he approached random people and chatted them up. Sometimes, they'd be annoyed. Other times, they'd get into a genuine conversation.

On a trip to Maine, we stopped at a restaurant for dinner after road tripping all day. It was late October, and the days were getting shorter and more depressing. After we finished our main course, out of nowhere a group of waitresses showed up, one holding a piece of cake with a lit candle on it. They all began singing happy birthday, looking at me. It would have been well and fun if my birthday didn't fall in March. Matteo looked at my puzzled and uncomfortable face and began to laugh. When the waitresses left the cake on the table and disappeared into the busy evening, Matteo grabbed a fork and said, "Dig in."

Various truths about Matteo began to emerge. Someone told me—maybe even he, himself—that he was once engaged to a black woman who was a professional boxer. Things didn't go well in their relationship. The storyteller didn't reveal why it had happened, but apparently, Matteo and his bride-to-be got into a physical fight one day, and she beat the crap out of him. Shortly afterward, he called off their engagement, and that was the end of his relationship with the boxer.

I began to connect these stories to his broken soul and the reckless behaviors currently revealing themselves, like a demon knocking at midnight and demanding to stay and party.

Our marriage had taken a bad turn, and I felt like I had lost our original path entirely. His behaviors and my disgust for him turned me off to the extent I didn't want to kiss or touch him anymore. Not that we'd ever kissed. At least not French kissed. I'd had a fear of French kissing ever since I was a teenager, and I never overcame that fear.

One day, Matteo decided we should have a session with his therapist, Stan, who he'd been seeing on and off for many years.

Stan lived in Newton, not far from Grandmother's place, and he held sessions in the office of his brick house that had beautiful curb appeal. He told us to sit down. He crossed his legs, looked at us both curiously, and finally asked, "So, what brought you here today?"

"We're here to talk about our marriage, our recent interactions. And hoping to get some help." Matteo said.

"What seems to be a problem?" Asked Stan. I was eager to share.

"I think Matteo gets annoyed by me often. For example, when I stand in one place, he'll walk toward me, instead of walking around, he'll stop and harshly tell me to move out of his way. It's not like I was *in his way*. I was just there. Why can't he walk around me?"

My opportunity to unleash my pain had finally arrived. As I described my issues with Matteo, a lightness came over me. I wanted to tell Stan much more. I wanted to tell him I was from Bosnia, and that the war had damaged me in a significant way. I wanted to describe the psychological impact of seeing my uncle killed. I yearned to go on to explain how hopeless my family felt when we lost our home. I wanted him to know that, as a Bosnian, I had left many more psychologically and mentally wounded people behind. I wanted to reassure him I wasn't the one still suffering; trauma permeated homes in Bosnia. I wanted him to validate my feelings and tell us both, as if the judge and the jury, Matteo was in the wrong. I needed Stan to be on my side. I needed him. As a psychotherapist, he needed to hear me out and understand that, back home, we needed thousands of vehement Stans to help eradicate our collective pain. And I wanted him to know that, at that moment, if he could carefully listen to me, listen to me for just a minute or two longer, he could easily become my hero and savior.

But this session turned out not to be about me at all.

After I had said my piece, silence filled the room. Stan looked first at Matteo and then me, as if he was measuring our character by the amount of conviction we brought, and would soon proclaim one of us as a suspect for crimes. Matteo was talking, Stan was responding, but I tuned out. Towards the end of the session, Stan finally said: "Matteo, I want you to come back see me. Alone. When is good for you?"

That was my first and only session with Stan. Matteo returned several times, but what his conversations with Stan entailed remained unknown. I was hoping his sessions with Stan would transform Matteo back to the person he'd been when I first met him, and that everything would go back to normal. But as time went on, the black cloud above us became darker and heavier.

## ❧ 7 ❧

# DECLINING DAYS

Grandmother was slowly falling into the cancer abyss, unable to eat, walk, drive, or do anything in which she'd taken pleasure doing before. She'd sit in her chair in the library, half asleep, with her head tilted to the side, drooling, unable to control her bodily functions. Her body had become so fragile that, when she woke up from her slumber, she'd slowly lift her head up, look around as if she'd just been born and begin familiarizing herself with her new environment. After taking high doses of morphine, she'd have episodes, hallucinating as if she was already in a foreign world, unable to connect with any of us anymore. I missed her.

I'd visit her in the library every opportunity I had, I'd sit next to her, gently taking her hand and caressing it. She'd open her eyes and, once she recognized me, she'd say: "Oh, hi, dear."

"Hi, Grandmother. How are you today?"

"Well, I'm in a lot of pain."

"Can you eat? Do you want me to take you to the kitchen?"

"I'm not hungry, dear. I don't have any appetite."

I didn't know what possessed me at the time, but I'd confess things about Matteo—the trouble we were going through—and

trying to reassure her that everything was going to be alright.-
Several feet from us stood a baby monitor, and through it traveled my voice up to the ears of Gloria who'd give us privacy by
spending time in the kitchen. When I was done with my confes-
sion, Gloria walked into the library and looked at me with the
eyes of deep empathy as if I were a little kitten she'd found abandoned on the street. I hadn't realized she'd listened to our
conversation.

Gloria's daughter and Matteo's cousin, Valeria, would visit
often from Pennsylvania and stay in one of the small rooms on
the second floor. We'd all sit in the kitchen and she'd call Matteo
*your uncle Matteo* as if implying he were *my* uncle. When she realized the mistake she had made, she'd shrug her shoulders, and
bring her hand to her mouth, with her eyes wide open in terror.

"Oops," she'd say.

When Grandmother was no longer able to walk up the stairs
to her bedroom, Matteo would scoop her tiny body from the
chair and carry her up the stairs to her second-floor bedroom.
For some reason, I wasn't allowed to follow, or come in to the
bedroom, so my goodnights always had to take place in the
library or in the hallway, watching Grandmother's little bald
head resting on Matteo's arm.

Suddenly, I was growing jealous of Grandmother, though no
fault of her own. I wished that Matteo would offer at least an
iota of his love to me, so I didn't feel like a loser, not deserving
any attention or love. But my feelings for Grandmother did not
change. As her body and mind departed her, I was there for
physical comfort and I attempted to radiate positive vibes to her
soul. She already looked like a living skeleton, and the only thing
that held her together was her beautiful spirit.

One morning, after many days of not eating well, I came to
her and said, cheerfully: "Grandmother, I want you to eat today.
You must eat. Do you hear me?"

To my surprise, Grandmother livened up, as if someone had

just woken her up from a bad dream, and yelled out: "Let's order a pizza! Papa Gino's pizza! Gloria, can you order us a pizza? Papa Gino's pizza!"

Gloria looked at me in disbelief and quickly picked up the phone to place an order for delivery. That day, Grandmother ate two slices of pizza, and we all watched her in awe, hoping she'd transform into the good old Grandmother full of energy and life. But two days later, early in the morning, Grandmother was found in bed, where she had already met her sweet angels. It was May, and the spring had already knocked on our doors, with the trees blooming along her large Greek revival home.

Gloria, Matteo, and I went to Mt. Auburn cemetery where Grandmother's body was cremated the following day. We waited on the other side of the furnace for her body to be placed inside. Her body had been delivered the day before, like it was a piece of furniture to be destroyed because it no longer functioned. The fire raged in the furnace and we heard the door open and her body slide inside. I put my hands up to my face as if to protect myself from this unusual scene. Soon, we'd hear Grandmother's bones crackle in the fire, sounding like fireworks on July 4. But much quieter. As her body turned into ashes in front of us, I silently said goodbye to Grandmother one last time.

Shortly afterwards, the funeral took place in a church in Newton Center. While her ashes stood in the middle of the altar, people came forth one by one to give a eulogy, describing Grandmother as the pillar of the family, the rock that stood proud and strong for ages.

Nothing would ever be the same again in the big revival home. I'd lost my best friend in America. I'd lost my only real confidante.

Her daughters were already on a mission to sell the house and disperse the proceeds of the sale amongst themselves and their children. Matteo never told me what his share of the inheritance was, and I never asked. Someone thought of me and decided to give me a couple of house plants that had belonged to Grandmother, and a black wooden pot stand with intricate details in faded colors. I took them in happily and imagined part of Grandmother's soul was living in the plants, watching and protecting me while I navigated an indifferent world. I'd water them, talk to them at times, and watch them, thinking of Grandmother's life that had followed a similar path to mine so many years earlier.

Years later, someone discovered and returned to me a letter I'd sent to Grandmother while I was still living in Bosnia. It said:

*SARAJEVO, BOSNIA-HERCEGOVINA*
*15. 04. 1997 (April 15, 1997)*
*My dear Teresa!*
*I decided to write you this letter but thinking about you whole time since we came back here to Bosnia. I hope you are very good as you seemed when I met you.*
*I want to congratulate you for your becoming great-grandmother one more time. As the child is growing up you can see how people get older very fast. The time goes really quickly that people are sometimes not conscious of that. But we have to know that we must live on the way the life gives us.*
*Grandmother, I want to thank you for everything, at first for accepting me to your wonderful house. I really had a great time, I was very comfortable and felt your warm friendliness. I am very glad that I met one wonderful, strong and friendly person as you are. Thank you very much!*
*Few days ago, on 12th of April the Pope John Paul II visited Sarajevo. That was his first time to visit Sarajevo and he was here for two days and the most of people in Sarajevo were very excited because of that big event. However, I think that is one of the greatest moments in history for my young country. He conducted a mass in front of thousands and thousands of people from all over the world. When he was leaving us, a*

*lot of people came out on the streets to see the Pope. Matteo and I came out, too, as we took some photographs of him.*

*Grandmother, at the end of my letter, I wish you all the best, and please take care of yourself.*

*Love you to you*
*From Nadija*

## ❦ 8 ❦

# REUNION

I have a pile of letters from that dark period, and when I recently pored over them, I wondered: who was Elizabeth? Who was Rebecca? Rebecca apologized in her letter for not writing me sooner, and complained her life was difficult and she wasn't feeling a hundred per cent. Where did I meet Rebecca? I can't recall some of these people who probably left my life as soon as they came.

Stacked in the pile are letters from my sister who was still contemplating getting an internet connection so we could exchange our notes via email. In the meantime, she and I would send handwritten letters as often as possible and recount our daily lives, our pain points and nostalgia for the times we used to spend together.

Shortly after I left, my father opened a grocery store on the ground floor of his mother's house, thinking that my sister Amra and her husband Anis would eventually take over and run the business. His idea would have been perfect had there not been two other grocery stores in close proximity, one literally next to my father's. Amra and Anis struggled. They didn't have a reliable car so most of the time Anis would carry the merchandise on his body.

Once in a while, they'd borrow my Uncle Hamo's car and take a few trips to procure the merchandise and store it in the corners of the grocery store. The foot traffic wasn't as robust as they would have liked. Amra complained in almost every letter how difficult and unprofitable the business was, and that she was tired most of the time. After her shift at the store, she'd go pick up Dženana from daycare, and then go home, cook dinner and get ready for the next day. And every day resembled the previous one.

In her letters, Amra mentioned that friendships had become fragile, people seemed distant, as if they had no interest in keeping their previous close relationships intact. She'd often say how difficult it was to find a person to have coffee with and to socialize. The palpable sense of community from before and during the war suddenly seemed to have fallen off a cliff, breaking into thousands of little pieces. Amra felt isolated and lonely.

So did I, in what I was calling my new home. I had a burning desire to connect with people, but every failed attempt made me more isolated. Rebecca could have become my new best friend. Elizabeth could have been a person with whom I could chat endlessly over a cup of coffee. But none of my relationships stuck. Was I wearing a friendship repellant? Perhaps, no one wanted to be associated with pain, to witness the aftermath of trauma.

Sometimes, feeling helpless, I'd try to open up to *anyone* who'd listen. Once time, I'd taken a cab alone for a braces check-up, and Dr. Diamond offered me a ride home. We got into a conversation about life and death, the topics that primarily occupied my mind. The conversation turned intellectual and deep, and I offered a piece of advice on how to live a life through pain.

"You know, Dr. Diamond, love cures everything. If people showed more love and kindness, I think everyone would be just fine."

Dr. Diamond looked straight ahead over the wheel, and at

the corners of his lips, I could see an attempt at a smile, but he didn't offer any opinions in return.

In the summer of 1998, a year after my arrival in the US, I bought a plane ticket to Sarajevo and visited my family for almost a month. By then, the grocery store had closed, and Amra and Anis had resumed their daily lives. Anis returned to the studies at the veterinary college that he'd halted before the war and hoped to land a job in a Sarajevo animal hospital as soon as he graduated. My mother helped Amra get a job at the TV station where she'd been employed herself for nearly three decades, a place where she knew the job and her colleagues inside and out. When the shop closed, Amra and Anis realized that their entrepreneurial spirit would never materialize.

Loneliness began to permeate our lives like sneaky animals crawling into our beds. In one of her letters, Amra told me she'd been sitting on the couch one day and started to cry because she was missing me. It was unconceivable for us to be separated now, given how much time we had spent together as children and teenagers. When Dženana saw Amra crying, she'd approach her and take her hand.

"Mom, why are you crying?" She still spoke in baby talk. She was only two.

"I miss Auntie Nadija."

"Don't cry, Mom. She will come soon."

I ARRIVED IN SARAJEVO ON A NICE SUMMER DAY AND FELT AS though I'd never left. I discovered my mother made *zeljanica*, a spinach pie, my favorite food, which had become an annual tradition thereafter. I wanted to know what I had missed during all the months I was gone. Had anything changed? Sarajevo now bustled with cars, a stark difference between empty streets during the war. Every night, I'd hang out with my friends, and they'd recount all the stories since I left Sarajevo. Melina, my war friend, told me about the U2 concert that took place a couple of months after I left.

"It was *the best* concert I have ever gone to. The energy was unreal." As she was explaining the experience in her intellectual way, I grew jealous that I'd missed it.

My mother recounted her story about President Bill Clinton arriving in Sarajevo shortly after I left for the USA. She decided she'd go to the airport and greet him, something Bosnians like to do when a person of special distinction visits the city. I probably would have joined her had I been there.

"I saw Clinton when he came out of the airport. I stood in a big crowd, and I'm pretty sure he looked at me." She offered her flirty smile, and I was happy to see it. She still had it in her.

My only significant story about things I'd discovered in the USA was a word previously unknown to Bosnians: Awesome!

"People like to say *awesome* there all the time." I announced, sounding young and naïve. If you said it in Bosnian language, *osam,* it means *eight*. We all liked this little vignette so much that we internalized it into a joke. Every time something went well or made us happy, we'd say, *devet*, which meant nine in Bosnian.

I had no other stories to offer up. I was afraid that my friends expected me to share exciting, Hollywood-style adventures about America. As I tried to construct stories in my head, I realized how little I knew about the culture or the people. I knew little even about my own new home and my husband. I had nothing to share but the uncomfortable stories I wanted only to conceal. I was afraid they'd laugh at me and say behind my back: *We told her not to go!*

I really wanted to be like a random person I'd once overheard at the Internet Café a couple of years back, talking about his life in New York City. He was sharing the same table with Jasmina and me, and he was accompanied by a couple of friends, describing the big city, telling of his adventures like he was in an action movie with all twists and turns. My own life had no shape. It was neither here nor there.

I followed my friends' lead, and they'd take me to different and new bars opened in Sarajevo. We made a trip to Mostar, the capital of Herzegovina, where a Pavarotti Center opened up the year I left. My friends, the drummers, had attended workshops and Jasmina and I would tag along. We rented a house in the Old Town and we'd party all night.

That's what I had missed. Carefree time among good friends and the love of my family. Soon enough, I'd return to the United States and continue my shapeless life.

## 9

# INDEPENDENCE EARNED

Right from the beginning, Matteo was in charge of our marriage. He was the captain of our sinking ship. He chose the direction we would go. We had no extensive conversations about our marriage, our future, and we didn't make mutual decisions as a couple. He made all the decisions by himself. Me? I felt like I was along for the ride, whether that ship was sinking fast or not. There was little compromise or choice at my end. I had to follow the captain.

Before I left for my trip to Bosnia, Matteo told me I would be better off living alone when I returned.

"I've been thinking about this a lot. Hear me out. It would be great for you to be on your own."

"Okay." I said. "Why?"

"It's the best way to learn independence and feel more comfortable. You'll discover a lot by living alone."

"Where am I going to live?"

"I asked Victoria to help you find a place."

"You did?"

"Yes. We already talked about it, and she agreed to help you."

"Okay."

As strange as the news sounded, I embraced the opportunity.

I didn't ask any more questions. I became convinced. Being more independent was not a bad idea, after all. I could then be Matteo's equal, or perhaps I could help navigate our ship and save it from sinking completely. I'd emerge as a better, more mature, readier wife—independent, knowledgeable, and strong.

When his friend Kachi came to visit a few days before I left Boston, I shared the news enthusiastically, repeating the same words Matteo told me:

"It will be good for me. I really need to become more independent."

"Yeah, sure," Kachi responded with a dose of skepticism.

Victoria helped find me a place to live and situate myself wherever I was going to land. They had come up with a plan to take me to Martha's Vineyard, where Victoria had lived a couple of decades earlier, finding a home on the tiny island off Cape Cod in Massachusetts. The morning she picked me up in her green beat-up Subaru, I had packed a duffel bag with clothes and other essentials. We put my bike on the rack at the back of her car, and made our way to the island.

Victoria was the eldest of the three sisters in the family. She was soft spoken, telling me stories about her life on the island back in her twenties. She had intentionally left home to find a new life, a better life, one she could be proud of. While living on the island, she enjoyed spending time on boats and she'd got herself a travel gig on cruises and yachts, living the life she'd always wanted to live. At some point, she met a guy and got pregnant. While she decided to keep the baby girl, she eventually cut the man out of their lives, and he never found out who his daughter was or would become.

I enjoyed hearing her stories, because they made me feel connected to her. I loved how she spoke honestly, with the straightforwardness that I was used to back home. She told me I would have a blast in Martha's Vineyard and advised me to have fun. I sensed she knew that Matteo and I had problems, but she never said as much, nor asked for details. Instead, she was patient with me; she only laughed when I showed anger at small things.

The ocean ahead of us appeared clear and vast when we arrived at the Steamship Authority at Woods Hole. The island protruded on the horizon. It was to be my new home, and I had no idea what to expect. We boarded the ferry, and the gentle waves became more belligerent at the ferry's forceful speed. As we approached the island, the ferry slowed down until it docked in at Oak Bluffs. *Welcome home.* People quickly rushed out of the ferry. I hesitated to move forward, fearful that my new home would be strange and unwelcoming. I looked at Victoria, and she gave me a happy smile that put me at ease. For now.

We dragged our bicycles and made our way to the house Victoria had found for me to live in. She had spoken to a friend on the island who'd thought of an old lady, the home owner, who had two vacant small rooms on the second floor of the house. She lived in Vineyard Heaven, not far from the Oak Bluffs center, a place bustling with busy tourists on foot, mopeds or bikes, looking for a good time and a place to relax.

We arrived at the house where the old lady's caretaker was waiting. She was a heavy-set woman, with shorter, permed hair, wearing sandals and denim shorts to her knees, with a button-down T-shirt. When I looked down, I noticed she had a tattoo on each side of her shin. Her voice was loud and obnoxious, carrying to all corners of the house, but nonetheless, she seemed friendly. While her name has escaped me over the years, my impression of her instant warmth and friendliness has remained.

"I come and see Mrs. B every day. I take care of her groceries, I make sure she takes her meds, and whatever else she needs. I'm here." She declared. "If you ever need anything to be comfortable, let me know, okay?"

We arrived at my room on the second floor. The second floor was smaller than six hundred square feet and my room was a little larger than the bathroom at the end of the small hallway between the two rooms. In my room stood a dresser on the left side, and a bed on the right, leaving some space in front of a window that offered a dull view of a busy street leading to the Vineyard Heaven center. At the corner of the long street was a movie theater and a few stores that sold expensive merchandise for tourists who could afford such things.

Victoria was to stay in the other room until it was time for her to go back home. When we unpacked, she took me back to Oak Bluffs to introduce me to my new boss who owned a jewelry store at the dockside. Steve was a man with a center parting, mustache, and an incredibly deep and loud voice that could be heard hundreds of feet away. I wondered if that voice had been cultivated intentionally to draw foot traffic into his store. For the most part, he didn't have trouble attracting customers, as the store seemed to always be busy with tourists eager to buy jewels in the shape of the island.

When we arrived at the store, he greeted us, unsmiling, as if immediately asserting his authority as my new boss. *War* and their familiar trumpet song "Low Rider" played in the background. Steve nodded and looked at me, taking stock of my character. In his deep voice, he greeted me.

"Hi, I'm Steve. How're you doing?"

He stared at me intensely and I imagined he was asking himself if I could handle the salesperson job, or if he could trust me, or if I were honest enough to handle his business. After introducing us, Victoria stepped outside and Steve and I were alone. The music still played in the background. Among the other store rules, Steve wanted music to be played at all times, but only from his collection of CDs. In addition, I had to clean the jewelry cases at least twice a day. Most importantly, he showed me how to work the safe that I would need to open every evening when it was time to close up and count the money for the day's sales.

At first, I felt overwhelmed with the responsibility of handling expensive jewelry. The safe looked enormous. But I also knew I was up to the task. As long as I followed the rules, I'd be fine. We agreed that I would start the following day, and I'd work two different shifts. Steve would pay me on a weekly basis, so I'd have rent money for each week. But the money was tight. While my rent wasn't much, my weekly paycheck could barely cover it, with only some left over for food and bus fare.

My days at the jewelry store were uneventful for the most part. I went in every day as expected and put a smile on my face for the smiling customers who wanted to treat themselves to new rings, necklaces, or bracelets. I felt a bit jealous that they could afford to buy these less-than-necessary items. I daydreamed about buying some of the jewelry and sending it to my mom and sister back home. They'd put it on, have something to remind them of me, and perhaps show it off to their work colleagues. *This came as a gift from America*, they would say. But I could barely afford to make a long-distance phone call to talk to them.

My biggest reward while working in the store came at the end of each shift when I said goodbye to Steve, hopped on my bicycle and rode down to the beach, not far from the bustle of Oak Bluffs Center. I'd arrive at the half-empty beach, jump in the ocean, and swim like a lonesome dolphin, happy to be in my habitat, but still missing my pod. As I swam along the coast, I was in my element. Swimming in the ocean reminded me of my childhood and trips with my family to the Adriatic Sea in Croatia, where I'd first learned to swim. My mom's cousin took Amra, me, and other cousins in a small boat far from the shore, and we swam around it like little ducklings. When my mom noticed our little heads protruding from the water in the far distance, she began to panic and violently started waving her arms signaling for us to return. But her cousin paid her no attention. He was a professional athlete and a certified diver and he had confidence in our ability as new swimmers.

Compared to the Adriatic Sea, the Atlantic Ocean looked like a monster about to swallow me. And this time, I had no protective eyes upon me. If the vast ocean took me away, no one would have known. My feelings of joy and sadness were entwined; this beautiful scenery should have led to happiness but instead I felt profound loneliness and confusion. I'd come out of the water and lie on the beach to soak up the sun. I'd imagine transcending into the world of joy—the kind of true joy I'd experienced growing up—with the people I loved the most. We'd laugh, share stories, and care for one another with the occasional hug. When the sun felt too hot, and I opened my eyes, I would see the yellow circle in the sky blinding my vision, telling me it was time to leave.

On my way home, I'd stop by a grocery store and buy myself enough food for the next couple of days. Mrs. B. barely used her kitchen, so she allowed me to cook there. I bought inexpensive food like cabbage and stew meat, then I boiled cabbage stew, packaging it for the following day to eat during my lunch break at the jewelry store. The smell of cabbage wafted through the hot air in the store; it'd smell like rotten hard-boiled eggs. It would linger for a while, because there was no breeze.

Steve couldn't help but make fun of my cabbage stew. He didn't care for the smell. I could tell he detested the idea of customers being diverted from the store due to the unappealing odor I had introduced. He'd go on and on about the smell—his occasional loud laughter carried outside—and then he'd share the information that cabbage was for the poor only.

"Fine, I won't bring it in again," I told him.

Having so little money, I spent most of my time in the tiny room at Mrs. B's. The kind of loneliness I had never felt before wrapped my days like an unwanted gift. It was worse than being a prisoner in solitary confinement. I still had freedom to experience the world, but the prospect of doing everything alone crushed me like a tsunami. For the first time in my life, I felt the weight of seclusion. My body and thoughts were for myself alone. I was like a lost child in a deep forest. I'd lie in my bed and look at the ceiling, the slated roof closing in on me like a casket that wouldn't let me go. I had no one to talk to. Mrs. B, who was both deaf and demented, minded her own business, and seemed to forget who I was every time she saw me.

My loneliness eased when I met Nora, a tan, tall and skinny woman who'd served in NATO in Bosnia for a little while right after the war. She'd heard from someone that I worked in the shop for Steve. News traveled fast on the small island, and she soon came over to introduce herself. She drove her little convertible VW Beetle and picked me up after work, then we'd go to the beach where we'd swim and grow more tan. I had no idea what Nora was doing on the island, nor did I ask. My ineptness, the voice that kept telling me I was a "stupid ignorant bitch" shut me off like a switch. I stayed quiet to make sure I didn't provoke that reaction from anyone again.

Nora seemed like a free spirit with a never-ending smile on her face. Her eyes squinted, even when she wasn't smiling or focusing. She worked at Jimmy Seas, an Italian restaurant sitting on a tiny hill in Oak Bluffs, that President Clinton once visited. His picture hung on one of the restaurant walls. With Nora's entrance into my life, my social circle slowly widened. I met her co-worker Mary, whose brother Chuck lived on one of the main streets in Oak Bluffs. I visited often and witnessed all of them showering in the front yard, which I found strange and un-American. I thought only people in developing countries like Bosnia would have outside showers. Chuck's roommate Justin eventually took me fishing, and I sat on the boat and soaked in the beauty and calmness of the ocean.

My new friends introduced me to a local bar, the Ritz, a place drenched in the smell of alcohol. There was live music every weekend, and the space would be filled with happy locals and tourists alike. I met Damian, a friendly bar bouncer whose mother was Japanese and father African-American. He was extremely attractive. When he conversed with people, his aura and confidence were apparent and undeniable. Damian always let me into the bar, fully knowing I was underage and should not be allowed into the bar in the first place. But every time he saw me, he gave me a hug and with a gentle tap on my back, he'd usher me in.

During my early days in the United States, I had a hard time accepting I could no longer go to a bar or a restaurant and order myself a glass of beer or wine. Having survived a war, I wouldn't have thought that indulging in small pleasures, such as having an alcoholic drink in a bar, would be taken away from me. Plus, how could a married woman be denied of such pleasures when her husband clearly could vouch for her, and tell those bar people, *she is mature enough. She is responsible. Let her have a drink.* But that never happened, which made me think that being married had no special privileges.

Damian was my new hero. I only visited the Ritz when he was there. He'd see me standing in line, looking at him like an innocent puppy waiting for a toy, and he'd raise his strong and muscular arm and wave for me to come closer. That experience of being "inside," of being accepted, of defying the norms and laws made the Ritz the closest thing to home. In my loneliness, I looked for opportunities to recreate my family, food, Sarajevo, Bosnia, but little came close and I often felt I'd failed. Cook like my mom—fail. Make friends similar to Jasmina—fail. Go out and party, meeting lots of people—fail. Call my sister at any time to hear Dženana's voice—fail. Instead, I stayed in my room, broke in both money and spirit, and stared at the ceiling, dreaming of new beginnings that I could grab once I figured out what my new home meant.

# 10

# NOMADIC LIFE

Just as my time in Martha's Vineyard started to feel more comfortable and my surroundings more familiar, with the predictable routine of working shifts at the jewelry store, my stay neared its end. All the locals who lived on the island year-round told me summer was the time they made all of their money, and when winter arrived, they fell into hibernation. Depression would ensue. Heavy drinking was rampant. Suicides had been known to happen. The island turned into a ghost town. Steve would inevitably close his store for the season, I'd lose my gig, and have to find my way back to my new, still unknown, home.

Before I moved back to the mainland at the end of the summer, I occasionally went back to Boston to see Dr. Diamond so he could tighten my braces and do a regular check-up. On such occasions, I'd stay a night in Grandmother's house and then find my way back to the island the following morning. After my appointment, Matteo and I went to a small bar, the Miracle of Science in Cambridge near MIT, and we'd sit across from each other like two strangers who had just met. At that point, I felt like we lived separate lives. My sure path to independence, like he suggested, was slowly being paved and I already felt a huge sense of accomplishment, a relief that I could live alone and earn money successfully, even if it was on an island that turned into death during the winter season.

We sat at a table and he sipped his beer while I had my Coke. This was no Martha's Vineyard. There was no Damian to rescue me, and the distance between this experience and home was growing vast and large. We stared at each other without saying a word, until Matteo grinned. He pursed his lips, as if he was mustering up the courage to speak, and finally said:

"So, what are your plans when you move back from the island?" I was immediately taken aback. Plans? I had not given any thought to my future plans upon returning to Boston. My focus was always on immediate goals: when to go grocery shopping, what to eat, when to visit the Ritz. My future prospects were blurred in managing day-to-day and barely getting by.

"I don't know. I'll probably need to get a job."

"Yes, that's always a good idea." When he was soft spoken, I knew he had something to say, to break some bad news that might devastate me, him, or both.

"I've been quite lucky so far in finding jobs," I was trying to show off the new independence I had paved for myself.

"I want to tell you that we're in the process of putting Grandmother's house on the market. We're working with a real estate agent now and we hope to sell it soon."

I had already learned that all house sale proceeds would be split between the two daughters, Gloria and Diane, and then the two would further split them between their children. Matteo would get a considerable portion.

"That's cool. I hope they sell it soon." I hesitated to say anything else, to presume I was somewhere in that picture as a new family member, as Matteo's wife. But Matteo didn't address any of that. Instead, he said:

"I think..." he paused. It was time to deliver the bad news, and I felt it in my gut as my eyes widened and my heart began to pound hard. "I think you should find another place to live when you come back from Martha's Vineyard."

Then silence came. I looked out the window, seeing students with their books quickly walk by like some random images flashing before my eyes. Not completely sure of my own senses, I asked him to repeat.

"Wait, what? What do you mean 'find my own place to live'?" He looked at me, guilt slowly steaming off of him as though from hot tea, and I could no longer see him from the cloud enveloping his increasingly repulsive duckface.

"I don't think we're meant to be together. I don't think we're meant for each other. I don't think we can live together. Now that we're apart, I've realized this, and I think we'd both be happier if we separated. At least for a little while. I'll help you find a place and settle in."

Instead of arguing, I went numb. I placed a shield around me to protect myself from potential pain, a defeat that would otherwise send me to an imaginary bottomless pit.

"Okay. I guess we can start looking for a place now. Because I only have a few weeks left before I return to Boston."

"Okay, I'll help you with that. I can help."

I realized that his idea to have me move to Cape Cod wasn't so much about my independence, as it was about his own.

NOW THAT I HAD TO FIND ANOTHER HOME, I RETURNED TO Martha's Vineyard, aware that my loneliness might extend indefinitely. Would I bear the consequences of my bad decision to marry and move to the United States indefinitely?

Back on the island, time continued as it had before. I began to save money more consciously, because I'd need it for rent in Boston. I only had three weeks to buckle down and double my earnings. I learned I had to put a deposit down for the first month and the last month—all this information was new to me.

It seemed like a lot of money, and I had to pick up a shift or two in order to save up enough.

Nora told me that Jimmy Seas, the Italian restaurant, was looking for a busser.

"What is a busser?" I asked.

"A busser is a person who helps the waitresses, you know. Bring bread and water to the table, clean up afterwards, stuff like that, you know."

"I think I can do that, but I've never worked in a restaurant before."

"Oh, it's easy, you can do it. You'll always have me around if you have any questions."

Soon after, I picked up a few nights a week at Jimmy Seas. The restaurant did quite well. Customers would wait in line, sometimes for an hour, just to taste the fresh pasta served in a pan. The smell of different sauces and garlic wafted through the air and enticed passersby. Even though the tasks seemed quite simple, I felt like I was put in the middle of a jungle and I couldn't find my way to the trees. When people sat down, I was so self-conscious I was afraid to even approach their table and set the bread on it. I imagined these hungry people would suddenly turn my way and start screaming at me for not picking up their glass as I should, or not bringing their bread on time. My fear of people seemed to be more evident as the opportunities to interact grew. I felt like a small person who shouldn't *take up space.*

*Stupid, ignorant bitch...* the voice often whispered in my ear. My fear only grew as I heard Jimmy, the restaurant owner, scream at his chefs and waiters to hurry, or not to mess things up. His voice was so loud the customers could hear him, but they minded their business for the sake of a delicious meal. Later, I learned Jimmy was using heavy drugs; it was his own way to cope and get through the busy nights.

But the extreme fear and anxiety didn't fully set in until one night. I went to a couple at their table and asked them if they wanted me to wrap up their leftover pasta. There was at least half a pan-full left, so they said yes. When I went to the kitchen to grab a box, I instinctively placed the pan above the trash and flipped it, releasing all the food into the trash can. When I realized what I had done, my blood froze. Oh no! I would have to pay for that in so many ways, I was sure. Not only would Jimmy scream at me, but they would let me go and ban me from the premises forever.

*Stupid, ignorant bitch!*

I went to Nora, crying. But she just smiled like it was no big deal, and that brought me a sense of relief.

"What should I do?" I asked.

"Go back to them, explain what happened, apologize and offer a free dessert." She sounded as if she had done this type of thing before.

My palms began to sweat and my heart started to beat hard. Could I muster the strength to approach the couple and tell them how badly I had screwed up, how much I had ruined their evening, and wasted their money? They'd probably never return again to the restaurant. When I approached their table, they were completely wrapped up in their conversation, enjoying themselves thoroughly and holding each other's hands. They barely noticed me. As I stood there awkwardly for a good ten seconds, they finally turned around.

I broke the news and offered free dessert, and they kept smiling, saying it was no big deal and rejected my offer for free tiramisu. And that was the end of it. It was that simple.

Relieved at this turn of events, I went home, tucked my money into the drawer envelope, and went to bed exhausted, physically and emotionally.

EVERY YEAR BEFORE THE WAR, MY FAMILY CELEBRATED EID. You couldn't call my parents religious Muslims, but their mothers followed the tradition and everyone partook in the cele-brations. For us, Eid was a time to get together as a family, share food, eat baklava. The day before the holiday, my mother would lay out our best clothes for Amra and me, and she would get us ready in the morning to visit my maternal grandmother for an all-day gathering, before we visited my paternal grandmother. On our way, we'd see the city, especially Old Town Sarajevo, as it bustled with men and their sons going to mosque for early prayer and marking the holiday as holy and special.

During Eid, both of my grandmothers would buy a lamb the day before, keep it in their yard and have it slaughtered by a professional at sunrise. Then that professional would cut the lamb into pieces, and my grandmothers would package those pieces in cellophane and get them ready for their grandchildren to distribute to the family and neighbors, as was the tradition.

This tradition was a big deal to me and my cousins, because we'd get gifts of money in return for the lamb. Our grandmother would place the wrapped-up lamb pieces on a tray, with a name tag on each one, and send us to the neighboring houses to hand them out. We'd knock on the neighbor's door, hand out a piece of lamb, kiss their hand (our grandmother would instruct care-fully whose hands we should kiss; it was for people my grand-mother regarded and respected the most), and they'd give us money.

One year, my older cousin Emir returned from one of his rounds, and as soon as he entered the room, he slammed the empty tray against the floor and began to cry: "Why did I get cheap neighbors? No one gave me money!" All the adults laughed. It was indeed bad luck for my cousin.

I lucked out and visited neighbors who were generous that day. I had collected a good amount of *dinar*, all paper bills I could save in a little purse I had kept beside me the whole time.

A few days later, I overheard my parents complaining about money. They were saying they didn't have enough to buy some-thing or other, and I resolved immediately to hand my Eid money to them. I was a saver. My sister was a spender. I was also a worrier who'd do anything to ensure my family was happy.

My parents didn't argue when I gave them my money. I could see relief and smiles on their faces.

"We will buy you something nice, Dikili." They'd nicknamed me Dikili at some point, a name that didn't resemble my own or anything that I had heard before.

"You know what, Mom?" I said proudly. "I'm so glad we're Muslim."

I FELT CONFIDENT THAT I'D SAVED ENOUGH MONEY FOR RENT when the time came. Every time I got paid by Steve or Jimmy Seas, I tucked it immediately into the envelope and put it back in the drawer. I had opened up a checking account at Bank of America, but I felt inept at using the ATM, and so didn't deposit my money into my account.

One night, I came home exhausted and didn't bother to put the money in the envelope right away. When I woke up the following day, I immediately got up and opened the drawer, only to be surprised that my envelope was not in its usual place. Was I still asleep and dreaming? I was pretty sure I had put my money inside it the day before. Did I perhaps put it in a different drawer? I frantically opened all the drawers to look for the envelope. I moved my clothes around, thinking maybe it got stuck somehow between my shirts or underwear, but every piece of clothing I moved yielded the same result; I could not find my envelope.

It struck me finally that someone must have walked into my room the night I was working my shift at Jimmy Seas. The perpetrator found the envelope and took it freely like it had been there just for them the whole time. Could Mrs. B. have done it? Mrs. B. was barely capable of walking on flat ground; I couldn't quite imagine her walking up a flight of stairs, half blind, rummaging through my drawers to take my money.

Baffled and lost, I called the police immediately. They arrived shortly after to investigate. Mrs. B.'s assistant heard the news (or maybe was she already there doing her daily check-up on Mrs. B.), but she happened to be at the house the same time the police did.

The two police officers told me they couldn't do anything about the missing money. They took finger prints on the drawers, saying it could help a little, but they made no promises the money would turn up. Mrs. B. appeared to be upset and shaken by police storming into her house. I was surprised to hear her adamant opinions, considering her quiet nature. But what was I to do? The stolen money was my only savings—a treasure I needed for my new home. If I didn't have that, I had no home. And my husband was pretty clear about the fact that he did not want to live with me. I needed to come up with something else, quickly.

The police officers, Mrs. B's assistant, and I walked outside and stood in front of the house, puzzled by the envelope's disappearance. *What could have happened? Who would have taken it? Why?*

I looked in the assistant's direction, and thought she looked nervous. Her storm of thoughts were evident from her furrowed brows; worry was written on her face. In my mind, I found her the only suspect. It had to be her. Who else knew I lived at Mrs. B's place or was familiar with the surroundings? She was the only daily guest, as Mrs. B's family lived far away. In my desperation, I began shouting like a wild animal that was about to bite:

"I am going to find this person who stole my money, and I am going to fucking make their life miserable!" I was as angry as a beast. But was I? Or was I just pretending, to scare her into admission. "And when I find them, they will pay!"

"No, no, no, no, no." The assistant was shaking her hand and arm in front of me, trying to calm me down. "How about I give you a check for the stolen money? How much do you think there was?"

I had no idea. Or I couldn't recall. My brain was shut off for a moment, and the amount I had earned was all but a distant memory. But I immediately calmed down.

"Oh, I don't know. Around a thousand bucks."

"A thousand bucks?" She repeated. She dug deep into her purse, gazing to her left side concentrating deeply as if she were about to draw a lottery ball. She found her checkbook and a pen and took them out from the purse, looking intently at me. "A thousand bucks, you said?"

"I think it was a thousand bucks. It could have been more, I don't know exactly." I wish I had known. Instead, she had me focused on spelling my name for her to write on the check. She handed it to me like we had just made a business deal.

"Here." She seemed more relaxed, the worry gone from her face.

I took the check and put it in my pocket, feeling defeated and spent. I was sure there had been more money in the envelope.

The following day, Mrs. B.'s children found out police had come to visit her house and were outraged that she'd been exposed to the scene of two cops walking into her home. They told me I had to vacate the premises immediately. But where was I to go? And why was I being punished for someone else's misdeeds? I had no choice in the matter. Still frenzied, I learned that Chuck at Oak Bluffs had offered to let me to stay in an empty room in his big house. He'd let me stay there for free until my days on the island came to an end. I packed my stuff and walked out the house, not even saying goodbye to Mrs. B. I sat on my bicycle and found my way to Chuck's, hoping my nightmare would somehow end soon. I felt like a nomad; Chuck's place would be my fourth residence within a year. The sole consolation was I had no furniture to move. It was only myself, looking for a permanent home that would welcome and comfort me. It pained me to think I had lost a home again.

I wanted to make my awful situation disappear in the blink of an eye, to be a small child again, saving my family from harsh days with my Eid money.

## ❦ 11 ❦

# SHEL

The proximity from Chuck's house to my two workplaces was quite convenient. I could walk down the street and find myself at work within minutes.

Since Chuck kindly offered me his home for free until my move back to Boston, I offered to do simple chores around the house, like washing the dishes, cleaning the floors, doing laundry, tidying up—anything that would make me feel less of a burden or a freeloader.

I continued bussing at Jimmy Seas, and my confidence in placing bread on the tables and filling up water in glasses had steadily grown over time. I felt comfortable doing the job. One night, Mary, another waitress, and Chuck's sister, cornered me at the restaurant and said, "You see that man over there, sitting at that table?" An older, bald man was enjoying his pasta dinner and a glass of red wine.

"Yes, I see him."

"He's wondering if you are free to go out for dinner with him soon." She smiled.

"What? Are you kidding me? Why would I go out with this man? That's insane."

"Do you even know who he is?"

"I... I don't know. I have never seen the man before."

"It's Shel Silverstein."

"Shel who?" I had not heard the name before.

"He's a famous writer. He's published so many children's books." She managed an envious smile.

"Well, tell him I can't do dinner with him. I can meet him for coffee tomorrow if he wants to." I left the restaurant as soon as I could, fearing I would have to face him that night.

When I arrived at Chuck's and told everyone I was going to meet Shel for coffee tomorrow, they were all amused and laughed.

"How cool." Someone said. "He could be your sugar daddy."

"Sugar daddy? What's a sugar daddy?"

"An old, rich dude who pays all your bills."

*An old, rich dude who pays all your bills?* Did my husband fall into that category? He was older than me. But was he rich? I did not have that information at my disposal. He was certainly paying the majority of our bills, but lately I had paid my bills alone. I refused the sugar daddy notion, hating to believe that I needed to depend on somebody else. I recalled it was my idea to go downtown and apply for a paying job at Macy's, as I'd rejected the idea of having a sugar daddy.

By the time the war had begun in 1992, I'd learned how to take care of myself. By the time I was fourteen, my parents' authority was essentially insignificant, while being shelled, with bullets flying around. Their daily advice became basic, falling into mere survival mode, and would often consist of these words: *Run fast! Don't go outside now! Be careful!* And all of that, to avoid being shot by a bullet or hit by shrapnel. As the war progressed, I became responsible for fetching water from miles away, for making bread, for learning how to cook. I eventually began interning at a barber shop, earning the scarce cigarettes that had become currency during the war.

Having a sugar daddy was not my MO. I despised the idea. When we lost our home in 1992 and returned in 1996, we found absolutely nothing in the apartment. The Serbs had taken all of our furniture. They'd driven the car away from our garage. They'd ripped out the bathroom and tore the kitchen fixtures apart and trucked them away like everything else in the house. We ended up escaping our home with a bag of audio cassettes, toothbrushes, and a few items of clothing. When the Serbs took over our neighborhood and stole our possessions, nobody in our family—except for my cousin Aida—came to our rescue to offer us a T-shirt, a sweater, or a pair of shoes. We scrambled, finding hideous clothes that had been left behind in empty apartments. The sugar daddy concept, as far as I was concerned, was synonymous to Santa Claus or a tooth fairy. None of them existed.

The following day, I found my way to Mocha Motts, a popular coffee place on Circuit Ave in Oak Bluffs, near Jimmy Seas. On time, as usual, I entered the coffee shop, and didn't find Shel there. I walked outside and waited underneath the stairs, next to the entrance door. As time passed and Shel hadn't shown up, I moved to the street and decided to casually stand there and look around, like I wasn't waiting for anything or anybody.

Out of nowhere, Shel appeared, wearing a long white garment, as if he was going to a wild toga party. He offered to buy me a coffee and I said yes, I would have a small one.

We headed to a large park with a tabernacle in the middle, an ocean view in the front and Steamship Authority on our left side. We sat on a bench overlooking the ocean, a wide distance between us both sitting on each end of the bench. After some small talk, I handed him a portfolio of the essays I had written during the ESL classes I took over the last couple of semesters. I wrote about my war experiences and about coming to the United States. Shel read with concentration, as if he just picked up a best seller. I suspected he'd start laughing at some point, like Uncle Keko's friend Kemo had laughed at my poems, but Shel kept a composed face and continued turning the pages until the end.

He closed the portfolio, looked out into the distance, and

began talking about the former Yugoslavia. I was impressed by his knowledge of it. I focused more on his raspy voice than the words he spoke. I felt his largeness, and sensed his intelligence emerge from him so easily. His imparted wisdom seemed dream-like and I enjoyed every second I spent with him. Then he took the two books he brought, and asked me to spell my name for him. In one book, he began drawing a tree in the shape of my name and a little bird dropping an egg next to it. It took him no time to finish the drawing. In the second book, he drew a large bird sitting above a box, with my name written inside it, a beak made out of the letter N. Next to it, he drew a flower. He signed both "With Love, Shel." He handed me the books and suggested we should depart. At one point, he stopped, looked out at the ocean, then finally looked at me.

"Listen. Don't let *anyone* fuck with your writing." He handed me a piece of paper and said, "Feel free to give me a call anytime. These are the phone numbers of my residences. If I don't pick up, leave me a voice mail message and I'll call you back."

I looked down and saw three different phone numbers jotted down. He said he moved around and spent time in different places; Martha's Vineyard was his summer residence. We said our goodbyes, and I turned to walk to Chuck's place, leaving Shel behind in my memory.

What was to come next, I could only have guessed.

# LONELINESS AFFIRMED

Returning from Cape Cod, I vowed that my life would be different, though not knowing whether it would be for better or for worse. While I spent my last days on the island, Matteo took the time to look for a new apartment for me until he found a suitable one.

Shea Road was near Davis Square in Somerville, between two busy roads, Holland Street and Mass Ave, with townhouses decorated with flowers at the front. One of those houses would soon be my new residence, which I would share with two other women. Matteo had found it and he took me there upon my return from Martha's Vineyard, so I could meet with the landlord and familiarize myself with the neighborhood. We arranged for me to move in immediately. Matteo managed to get a futon, which was the only piece of furniture I now had. I also had a telephone which I placed on the floor.

My new landlady, Vanessa, was a short Asian woman with dark hair and a strong personality. The morning I moved in, she, Matteo, and I sat at the kitchen nook discussing the house rules. When it came to deciding which type of lease to sign—month-to-month or one-year—an argument ensued. Matteo insisted upon a long-term lease, whereas the landlady was firm on having month-to-month. The argument turned into a shouting match, and I just sat there, not knowing the difference between the two. Vanessa finished the argument by making it clear she was the landlady, and she was the one to make such a decision. Matteo, fuming, stood up and headed for the door. I followed him outside to say goodbye. He instructed me not to sign anything if she handed me any piece of paper in the next couple of days. I assured him I wouldn't.

He left, and I resigned myself to spending time in my room alone. I ventured to the kitchen and eventually met my two roommates. Anna was a student at Harvard, originally from Venezuela—or was it Colombia? She was short and her curly hair looked like a wig on her small, rounded face. Her teeth looked like baby teeth, and there was a gap between her two upper front ones. Every time she smiled, I'd stare at the gap. She was friendly, but she always appeared to be busy and had no time for anything but her studying.

I was hungry for company. In Bosnia, I would never be alone with my family around. Now, I would do anything to grab Anna's attention for even a few minutes, talk about things, share intimate stories, laugh, drink coffee like I did back in Bosnia with my family. But Anna showed no interest. She'd come to the kitchen where I'd often sit at the nook. She'd say hi and make her bowl of rice with a side dish. She'd take the bowl with her and go to her room, leaving me alone like a drooling animal hungry for a meal.

My other roommate was just the same. She was a white girl with a professional job, a bit heavy with shorter blonde hair. Her room stood right next to the kitchen. Her boyfriend, a tall and friendly fellow, would visit often and they'd have the loudest sex I'd ever heard. She would scream and scream, and the whole house would echo with the sound of her orgasm. I'd run to my room, slam the door behind, and try to ignore the sounds. The following day, she'd see us in the kitchen, without saying anything, or apologizing, or having decency to inquire whether we minded her loud sex.

A few days after the incident between Matteo and Vanessa, she showed up at the house with paperwork and asked me to sit down at the kitchen nook to sign it. I assumed everything was in order, like they'd discussed and agreed upon. I barely read what it said, but Vanessa kept insisting.

"Here, sign it." She put the papers on the table and shoved them in my direction. "Sign here." She showed with her finger where to place my signature. I took the pen and quickly signed my name and shoved the papers back in her direction. She separated them into piles and handed me one.

"Here is your copy." She then stood up and left.

I informed Matteo over the phone that the lease was signed and all set.

"What does it say on the front? What kind of lease is it?" I felt the tension in his voice, and it kicked me into anxiety mode.

"It has my name on it and the price." I said.

"No, no, no. That's not what I'm asking. What kind of lease is it? It should say if it's one year or month-to-month." I looked more carefully, trying to push my anxiety away so I could focus.

"It says month-to-month."

"Damn it! I knew it! That bitch tricked you into signing the lease. I told you not to sign anything, didn't I?" Silence. "Well, okay, we will see what happens. Just don't sign anything else if she asks you, okay? She can't kick you out."

We hung up the phone, and I still didn't understand what it all meant. Month-to-month had been my normal way of living once upon a time. During the war, it was more like minute-to-minute. You never knew if you'd survive.

Talking to a human being over the phone, even though it was anxiety-provoking, felt like a reprieve. Most of the time, I was alone. My phone never rang. I tried calling a couple of people I'd met in Martha's Vineyard, but no one ever picked up. I considered leaving a voice mail message, but I had nothing to say, nothing to offer. Hoping they might have seen my missed call, I imagined they might call me back, but those calls never came.

When I returned from grocery shopping at Stop and Shop in Porter Square, just a mile or two down the street from my house, I put away my groceries in the kitchen and ran to my room to check my phone for voice mails. And same old—nothing. Days had gone by, and Matteo didn't call me either.

The four walls of my room closed in on me, and as soon as darkness arrived, I felt the ghosts of loneliness flying around my head. I was so scared of my own presence, of the emptiness that permeated my space, my mind, and my soul. I was afraid to leave the room and venture out, because the world seemed unfair and unkind. Every day I spent alone, my loneliness multiplied to infinity. I felt my soul floating above my body, the two entities estranged and separated. My identity was slipping away and I no longer knew where my future was taking me. But every once in a while, the survival instinct that had carried me through the war knocked on my door and demanded I do something with my life. I was determined to escape the walls of the dark room and step into the other side of this beautiful and promised land.

## ❧ 13 ❧

# WHAT IS HOME?

It was 1998. At the beginning of autumn that year, I was starting to notice the foliage changing in New England. Some said it was one of the most beautiful scenes in the country.

For the first time, I realized how beautiful the streets of Cambridge and Somerville were. Leaves from the trees lining the side streets were turning bright red and yellow, their colors melting with the sunshine. The transformation of the leaves signaled the cold and long New England winter to come, and I was not sure I was ready for it. I had to keep myself busy somehow.

On a cool day, I found myself in Harvard Square looking for a job. I arrived at the front of the Harvard Science Center and approached a billboard bearing different advertisements. Someone told me that term positions were often promoted like this. I looked carefully to see if anything suitable was listed, and noticed:

*Prep room, Science Center basement*
*Looking for an audio-visual scheduler*
*Starting immediately*

That seemed interesting, possibly photography related. I had lost interest in pursuing photography long term when I realized it was an expensive and competitive endeavor. But I was hoping my love for the art form would still motivate me to land a job in the field at some point. As I already had some experience working in the stock agency, I might be qualified for this role. Since I was nearby, I decided to find the place and inquire about the job. The Science Center looked like a big concrete box, oddly shaped, with two revolving doors and one regular door on the right. I entered and headed to the basement, following the signs for the prep room. The hallways leading to the room looked dark and uninviting.

When I entered the room, I was greeted by a man at the front desk who told me I'd have to speak with José, the manager of the prep room. He picked up the phone and dialed, letting him know I was there.

José soon appeared from the corner of the room, where stairs led to the upper floor and his office. He was a skinny man, who wore glasses and his hair parted in the middle. He dressed in khaki pants and a vest over a shirt. He had a slight accent, which put me at ease. We exchanged a few words, and then he asked me what experience I'd had with audio visual equipment, and whether I'd had any computer experience.

"Yes, I have a computer at home." I lied. "Plus, I can learn quickly." He showed me what the job entailed and it looked simple enough. My job would be to ensure any classes and reading sessions held at Harvard would receive audio visual equipment as requested by a professor or a research assistant. I'd track the inventory, place an order, answer the phones, and check emails on a regular basis to ensure all requests were being answered in a timely manner. That seemed easy enough. I told him I could do the job and I could start immediately, perhaps tomorrow. He appreciated my enthusiasm, but instead of saying I'd got the job, he asked me to fill out some paperwork with my information, and then he'd give me a two-week trial period to see how things went before the position became permanent. I obliged. I'd do anything to stay away from my dark room at home. He told me to show up at one o'clock the following day, and to take a second shift serving the reading sessions, which could go on until nine pm.

At the same time, I enrolled in an Intro to Psychology course, an obvious choice for me, that I hoped would help alleviate the heaviness of my current life. Maybe I'd learn how to cope better by learning new theories and ways to alleviate sadness, anxiety, and depression—the main themes of my life. After my first class, in which the professor gave us the syllabus, I headed to the COOP, a Harvard book store that sold textbooks for every school within the university.

I found the psychology section and carefully picked out the books listed in the syllabus. I picked out a heavy textbook and *The Ego and the Id* by Sigmund Freud. I went home and pored over the pages, trying to absorb the words and understand the subject matter. A few weeks later, when the professor began the book discussion, I realized he hadn't mentioned any of the concepts I'd read about. I grabbed the syllabus to see if I had missed something and realized I had bought the wrong book by Freud. The syllabus clearly stated *Five Lectures on Psycho-Analysis*. The following day, I went to the COOP and exchanged the books, but when I began reading the other one, I could barely understand any of concepts written. Psychology was proving more difficult than I'd expected. My hope that it might help me resolve my problems seemed to have been a delusion. I felt ever more inept and awkward, making the simplest mistakes. If I couldn't choose the right book, what could I expect? Was my mind so messed up that I couldn't even do basic functions? I felt lost in the darkness and, in my loneliness, I couldn't see a way to the light.

OCTOBER UNFOLDED, AND THE DAYS AND NIGHTS TURNED cooler. I'd do shifts at the prep room, and make a living at minimum wage. After work, I'd go to class once a week then promptly go home to where the dark room and empty voicemail box awaited. One night, I saw an envelope bearing my name in unfamiliar writing, sitting on the kitchen nook. For a second, I cracked a smile because getting mail always made me happy. Ever since I'd moved to the United States, I'd regularly exchanged letters with Amra. Occasionally, I'd receive a letter or a postcard from another friend, and I'd read them several times in a row, study the letters, wonder how they felt when they were writing it. A few days before Thanksgiving, a postcard from Steve, my old boss in Martha's Vineyard arrived in my inbox, wishing me happy holidays. At the bottom, he wrote: "P.S. Are you making cabbage for Thanksgiving dinner?"

I was not looking forward to Thanksgiving that year. When I headed to work one day, I stood next to the bus driver, and she asked my name, where I and my accent had come from. I embraced the opportunity and began telling her about Bosnia, how I'd left my family behind, and that now I lived all alone. After hearing my stories, she asked, "Where are you spending your Thanksgiving this year? Are you going anywhere?"

"I think I'm just going to stay home," I replied.

"You can't stay home alone for Thanksgiving! Unacceptable. I'd love for you to come to my place and celebrate with me and my family. You shouldn't be alone, no."

When we came to the last stop at Harvard Square, she pulled out a piece of paper and a pen and wrote down her address and a phone number. She handed it to me and said, "I look forward to seeing you. Come any time on Thursday! We will have fun."

I grabbed the piece of paper and with some hesitation, I said, "Okay, thank you."

I stepped off the bus, with mixed feelings about this encounter. On the one hand, I was grateful that people like her existed. On the other, what if she were a serial killer and invited me to her house to murder me? Who would find out? Who would care? I hated the four walls of my room, but at the same time they were my protection from the world.

That protection didn't seem to last. When I opened up the letter sitting on the kitchen nook, I realized the landlady had sent me an eviction notice. She had exercised the rights to do so contained in the month-to-month lease. She was giving me a month to move out, which fell at the end of November, just as Thanksgiving wrapped up. The four walls of darkness were coming to a strange end. But where was I to go next? Life had just presented me with more uncertainty. But I had to move forward.

BACK IN BOSNIA, MY PARENTS WERE GETTING READY TO MOVE back to their old home. The rubble from the war was forming once again into livable space.

In June 1992, my neighborhood, *Aerodromsko Naselje*, or the Airport Neighborhood, had been occupied by the Serbian paramilitary group *Orlovi*, Eagles, who'd taken our neighbors away to concentration camps. They separated women and children from the men, and they brutally killed seventy-four of our neighbors on the spot. My family and I ended up at my aunt's place in Dobrinja Five, a neighborhood a ten-minute walk away from our home, where we spent the rest of the war. In July 1992, we moved to an empty apartment that had belonged to a Serb family with two small children. They had escaped in the beginning of the war and went to the Serb side. We called their old home our new home.

The war ended in November 1995, and by March the following year, we'd learned that the Serbs had to give up our neighborhood and hand it back to the Bosniaks. We couldn't wait to go back and see what remained of our home. We'd hoped that at least our photographs would have remained intact, or I'd find my poems and stories. The day we returned, however, we found nothing but endless rubble in front of our desperate, sad eyes.

Our home had been looted. When my father realized his car had been stolen, he kept complaining to my mother they had made a terrible mistake in not taking the car with them. He'd been complaining about it through the entire war. But my mother, always rational and practical, reminded him the car would probably have been damaged by numerous bullets or shell shrapnel from the very beginning of the war, or confiscated by the Bosnian Army.

"Besides, where would you go with it? Where would you get gasoline? Come on, Munib, don't talk out of your ass." She'd always say that to try and talk sense into him.

While her sharp tongue sounded a bit harsh at times, she was right. No one could argue with her. Sarajevo was under siege for the entire war, and we had no way to escape or go anywhere. My mother was right most of the time. Even with only a high school diploma, she displayed strength and intelligence; she was admired by her friends and colleagues for her street smarts and wit. During the war, she kept us all alive by cooking under the most trying conditions, or washing laundry with little water.

In the ESL class I took when I first arrived in the United States, our instructor asked each student to come up with a personal hero, and explain, in the best English possible, their choice. Some students would say Batman, some would say another fictional character, or a character from their favorite book series. When my turn came, I said proudly and loudly,

"My mom. My mom is my hero." Next time I talked to my mother on the phone, I told her this story, and she burst into tears. I hated it when my mother cried. I had seen cry her so many times during the war. Her pain was so deep and etched into her soul that it had replaced the loud laughter she had been known for before the war. She was reduced to feelings of sadness and hopelessness at times. When I sensed she was deep in thought as I talked to her, she would blink multiple times—one slow blink after another—as if to bat her thoughts away.

The distance between us seemed surreal at times. As my life in the United States was unfolding in unpredictable and unusual ways, I tried to remain positive for her so I wouldn't give her any more reason to cry. I concealed my discomfort and suffering so I could protect her. But a good piece of news arrived in September, a reason for my family to be happy. On October 2, 1998, my parents would be able to return home to *Aerodromsko Naselje*. Humanitarian aid from a number of countries had arrived in Bosnia after the war, and people had worked hard repairing the infrastructure destroyed by the war.

They'd have to start buying furniture from scratch, well into their late forties and early fifties. For a Bosnian family, that would have been unheard of before the war. None of that mattered since my parents preferred to return to their old habitat, even though it would never be the same as before, instead of occupying Serbs' old apartment.

"It won't be the same, but at least we know it's ours," my parents would say. It would never be the same again. Our neighbors had scattered to different parts of the globe; children that used to play on the streets, making loud noises along the buildings, were now grown-ups, finding their way to a better life; the streets were now scarred with mortar marks and bullets, a reminder of the brutality and death; the airport was quieter and less busy, a sign the economy still didn't function at full capacity; ghosts were flying around, trying to forgive and forget. But still. Home was theirs.

It took me a while to realize that my survival mode had extended indefinitely. Living in a foreign country and finding my way around was now survival. Like back in Bosnia during the war, I had no home of my own. My future looked muddy, worse than a polluted river. Here, I had no friends or family members to turn to. I was living like a newborn, trying to gasp for air at first sight of the world, relying on someone else to feed me, clothe me, give me love. Time was a slow ticking clock, the movement of each hand anticipating perhaps death, or dying or, in this case, even worse—the death of the soul. Surviving was not living. To move out of survival and into another mode of existence, having a home, was a good start.

While my parents were happily settling in their old home, I was still searching for my new one.

## 14

# COUNTLESS MOVES

When I told Matteo that Vanessa, my landlady, was evicting me, he was pissed.

"I knew this bitch would kick you out! Unbelievable."

"What should I do?" I heard panic in my voice. "Where should I go?"

"We will figure something out, don't worry." Matteo was my only problem solver. I had no one else to guide me or give me advice on the next steps, and direct me to places where I could look for a new home.

Days went by without any resolution. I focused on school and going to the prep room for my shifts. Al, my colleague, often whistled as he moved the audio-visual equipment around, and my body would cringe like a thousand little bugs were crawling on my skin. I hated it. Al was a happy-go-lucky guy in his mid-thirties, who liked to chat with the daily visitors, mostly students who asked for help in setting up the equipment. When he talked, I noticed his lisp, and the way he pronounced the *S* had a certain ring to it that echoed in my head for a long time. I'd run out of the room and take a walk to the cafeteria on the first floor, sit down and watch students place fried chicken and pizza slices on their trays. Then I'd go back, hoping Al had disappeared and gone to his small corner cube where he'd do whatever he did in his spare time.

A Harvard student group would often book a movie to be shown in a large amphitheater in the Science Center, and someone at the prep room would run the projector and switch the reels at the necessary time. One evening, the student who usually did it wasn't available, so Al asked me to stay around to do it. He showed me several times how to switch the reels, by pushing the levers when the third little dot appeared on the upper right corner of the movie screen. The dot was the signal it was time to switch the reels. I had to watch the movie intently or I'd miss the task.

When the night came, I set everything up in the booth looking over the entire amphitheater and the large screen in the front. A number of students showed up and took a seat. At exactly eight pm, I began projecting the movie and everything went as smoothly as it should. About fifty minutes into the movie, I began watching for the dots to appear and when the third finally showed up, I pulled for the lever. But something got terribly stuck and I wasn't able to switch the reel. I tried again and again, but the reel refused to get into the gear for the movie to continue. And then—a black screen. I heard the students booing, and my palms began to sweat uncontrollably. *Oh no, what I am going to do now?*

*Stupid, ignorant bitch!*

I blacked out and my mind stopped working, failing to come up with a solution.

Suddenly, the booth door opened up and there stood my other colleague Jeff, a short man with mustache and beard, wild hair and eyeglasses. He appeared as if sent as a gift from heaven, and I wanted to give him a big hug for coming to my rescue.

"I heard the students booing," he said.

"I'm so sorry." I was on the verge of tears. He remained calm. "Don't worry. It's not like it hasn't happened before. We'll fix this." He came up to the projector and pushed the levers with ease. The screen lit up with the next movie scene. The students became quiet. But for me it was another failure, even if small and insignificant. I went home, knowing I would never handle a movie projector again.

I received a phone call from Matteo the following day. I'd often tried to call him, but he was difficult to get hold of, and I would never leave a voicemail message.

"Listen, for right now, I think you should move in with me." By then, Grandmother's house had been already sold, and Gloria had moved back to Pennsylvania, her permanent residence. Joe, the Amish-looking man, and the Boston College student must have found a new home. Matteo found an apartment in a two-family house in a part of Newton called Nonentum, predominantly filled with Italian Americans. The traffic lines on a few streets were painted the color of the Italian flag—green, white, and red—instead of the usual yellow.

At the end of November, leaves had already left their trees, and the chill was starting to settle in the air. The day Matteo picked me up, the weather was crisp but sunny, and my room was lit with early sunshine. It was a Saturday. He picked up a small U-Haul truck on his way, to carry the futon, my only possession.

As we moved my things from the room to the truck, my housemate Anna walked by, looking angry, not paying attention to either one of us. She walked into her room and slammed the door. Matteo went up to her door and knocked.

"Anna, Anna, open the door," he pleaded.

"No! Just leave me alone," she replied.

"Anna, I want to talk to you. Open the door please." But Anna remained unresponsive and silent.

*What just happened?* I had no idea what to make of that scene. Why was Anna angry? And why did Matteo want to talk to her so badly? What had I missed? The scene between the two people who had seen each other only once before seemed too strange. But I didn't ask. I had other, more important things lingering in my mind. What would my new home, my sixth residence in less than two years look like? What did living with Matteo again mean? Why had he changed his mind about living with me? Would our troubled marriage improve? What would it look like from now on?

We left Shea Road without saying goodbye. I'd never see Anna again. I'd never find out what that commotion was all about and why Anna was so upset. On our way to Nonentum, I looked through the window of the U-Haul truck and observed the neighborhood. The roads Matteo was taking without any directions had not become familiar yet. If you'd dropped me off in the middle of the street and told me to find my way around, I'd have immediately gotten lost.

I clenched my hands, feeling my palms sweat. While silence permeated the truck, it dawned on me that in this deeply rooted loneliness, the only person I could rely on for my survival was Matteo. My life rested in his complex, dirty hands, and I felt like I had no choice but to give in.

THE APARTMENT IN NONENTUM, MY NEW HOME, WAS OWNED by an old Italian lady, Margarita, who lived in the house next to ours with her son, Vinnie. I learned later they made a living from real estate (they owned several houses in close proximity) so Vinnie had been unemployed for years and was hanging around the house all day, every day. Our house was a two-family house sitting on the corner of a busy street connecting Watertown and another street leading to other parts of Newton. Traffic seemed to flow constantly. Just a block away, I could catch the bus to Watertown Square and take the trolley bus to Harvard Square, where I'd continue my classes and work at the prep room.

The apartment consisted of three small bedrooms, joined by a short and narrow hallway covered in unappealing dark brown carpet. At the end of the hallway was the bathroom. On one side was the dated kitchen with an old, brown stove in between ugly and uninviting kitchen cabinets. Matteo's brother Fabio had found a kitchen table sitting on the side of a road and snatched it, eventually giving it to Matteo for his new home. The table only had space for two chairs, and Matteo had found a couple of mismatched ones and placed them on either side of the table.

We never we used the front door of the house, we always climbed up the steep and long stairway at the back that led to a small porch and the kitchen door. We entered the house backwards; everything else in our life seemed backward, too.

By the time I moved in with Matteo, he had already picked up a new hobby—skiing. He'd leave the house early on Saturday, stay over the weekend and return on the Sunday evening. Shortly after I moved in, his brother Fabio came to pick him up in his red pick-up truck. They didn't bother to invite me or even consider it, so I broke into tears like a small child being separated from her favorite toy. Fabio came into the kitchen waiting for Matteo, and in witnessing my reaction, he shook his head, turned around, and told Matteo, "I'll wait for you outside."

He walked out without saying goodbye.

Matteo left, and I returned to my loneliness. When I found myself alone in the house, the phone would ring frequently. When I picked it up, there would be silence on the other end and then the caller would hang up. We got those phone calls every day. I told Matteo about them, suspecting he might know who they were coming from. One day, when he came home from work, he promised the calls wouldn't happen again.

When he returned from skiing, he told me I should sign up for a drivers' ed class, learn how to drive, and get a license. In his mind, he probably thought that driving would give me freedom to move around and be independent. But I still had nowhere to go and no one to visit. The closest drivers' class he could find was located at Brookline High School, a short bus ride from our house. He signed me up and, right away, I found myself immersed in driving lessons.

I'd first learned to drive first back in Sarajevo when Matteo took a chance with me once and drove us to Vrelo Bosne, a national park below Mount Igman—one long straight road surrounded by tall trees. He showed me how to push the clutch and switch gears in his company's Jeep and then he'd stop in the middle of the road so we could trade places. Following his instructions, I would place the shift stick into first gear and slowly push the accelerator. We moved slowly and I'd zig-zag along the road, making a driver behind us angry. He opened up his window and started screaming at us, so we'd stop and trade places again in order to clear the way for the angry driver.

Matteo was a good driver, but he was impatient. If someone didn't move at the pace he expected, he'd make a sharp turn, go around them, and leave them in the dust. His boldness wasn't always appreciated.

Before we moved to the United States, Amra, Anis, Matteo and I decided to go on a short trip to Dubrovnik, one of the most popular tourist sites in Croatia. The roads on the way were winding, and with every turn you'd pray not to collide with anyone or drive into the Neretva River below. Matteo showed off by driving fast and taking those turns as though he was driving in Formula One. Suddenly, a BMW passed us and then slowed its pace in front of us. Matteo didn't appreciate this move, so he tailgated the car, getting as close to him as possible. The BMW driver stopped suddenly in the middle of the highway. The driver's door opened, and the man, muscular, wearing a pair of jeans, a T-shirt, and aviator sunglasses, walked toward us. For all we knew, he could have had a gun and been ready to shoot us had we confronted him. The war had just ended, and the rage of the aftermath was starting to unfold. We suspected there were plenty of madmen showing their ugly side, walking and driving around.

Instead of confronting him, Matteo began shaking his head to signal that he didn't intend to be mean. He put the shift stick into reverse and began driving backwards. When the man saw that Matteo was capitulating, he walked back to his car, and as soon as he entered, took off. Anis got excited.

"We should have beat up this motherfucker." As a soldier during the war, he had war demons on his shoulders and was easily triggered. Matteo laughed out loud at Anis's remark. Amra and I sat in the back of the car, nervously laughing, watching the scene unfold in front of our scared eyes.

After that experience, Matteo was more careful when he drove in Bosnia. As soon as we arrived in Boston, he became emboldened again and returned to his old self.

MY DRIVING INSTRUCTOR WAS A SHORT MAN WHO WORE eyeglasses, in his late forties or early fifties. He held classes in a Brookline High School classroom and then he'd arrange a driving lesson with each student. Mine usually took place at the weekend, for an hour or two at a time. He sat next to me and instructed me to take a right, take a left, go straight, push the brakes, make a full stop. He asked me what the signs we encountered meant. He usually took me on Route 9 and then we'd make our way to the high school on side streets. As far as I was concerned, everything was going smoothly and my driving confidence was growing. I could do it, and nothing could stop me. When the time came to take the written test, I passed it with flying colors. The instructor scheduled a road test with a state police officer for me at the Registry of Motor Vehicles.

The police officer looked frightening, with his stern face and a gun hanging on the side of his belt. Guns scared me and provoked my anxiety—one of my emotional souvenirs from the war. I tried to look past and ignore it, to focus only on one thing: I had to pass this test. We both sat in a car and then he instructed me to go straight, take a left, go straight again, take a right, take another right, until we came to a full circle and ended up where we started. My instructor was patiently waiting outside for the outcome. The state trooper and I got out of the car, and then he walked to my instructor and handed him a piece of paper. Then he walked away.

The instructor looked down and when he read it, he informed me I had failed the test.

"Why did he fail me?" I was surprised. I thought my driving was impeccable.

"The note says you didn't come to a full stop at the stop sign."

"What do you mean I didn't come to a full stop at the stop sign? I don't get it." I insisted.

"What he meant is you didn't sit at the stop sign long enough before you proceeded to take a turn."

"That's total bullshit, that's bullshit!" I started to cry and I turned around, walking as fast as I could. I heard his voice behind me.

"Wait! Let's talk, don't just leave like this. Wait." But I didn't stop. I kept walking until I arrived at the bus stop, fuming at the injustice that had just taken place.

A few days later, Matteo and I were walking around Newton Center, finding a place to grab a bite. At a corner of the street we were about to cross, I noticed a police car take a turn, without making a stop at the stop sign.

"Look at this asshole! A cop just failed me for not stopping at the stop sign, and look at this guy! Is he allowed to break the rules because he's a cop?" I was clearly triggered. The walls of injustice were falling down on me, and I didn't hide my feelings of rage. The police car parked on Centre Street, and the police officer stepped out of the car just as we crossed the street. Matteo came up to him.

"Excuse me, officer." He showed no reservations about speaking up when it came to addressing injustice. "My wife here... she noticed you didn't stop at the stop sign, and just a few days ago, the state trooper failed her on her road test because apparently she didn't come to a full stop." Awkward silence occurred. The police officer looked at us and, like everyone else we encountered, he must have wondered how we ended up being a married couple. He cracked a smile.

"Your wife is absolutely right. I should have stopped at the stop sign, and I apologize for not doing it. I'll try to be more careful from now on."

Had I heard that correctly?

"Why, thank you, officer. We appreciate it." Matteo said.

The next time I took the road test, I passed. I got my temporary license, and soon after, Matteo and I went to the Boch Toyota dealership in Norwood. Matteo put a down payment on a car, and I covered the monthly payments. We ended up driving away with a used red Toyota Corolla, which was to be my new outlet to freedom.

## ❧ 15 ❧

## SAD NEWS

I was sitting at my desk in my office one day when Matteo rushed in with a piece of paper in his hand and said, "Nadija, I just found out that Shel died yesterday."

It was May 11, 1999. Shel Silverstein had died the day before.

"I am so sorry." He handed me the piece of paper, a printout from the Internet, with Shel's obituary.

When I first told Matteo I had met Shel, he'd been excited.

"You should give him a call and keep in touch with him."

I tried to call Shel only once, using all the three numbers he had given me, but I had no luck reaching him. I didn't leave a voice message.

"I'm so sorry." He sounded as if he was offering his condolences for a family member or a good friend. I felt numb and emotionless.

My dealings with death and dying took a different shape during the war. Surrounded by civilian casualties almost every day, I'd witnessed people losing their limbs or their lives in front of me. Those deaths were associated with long and painful screams, asking for help before realizing help was limited. When a shell fell on the street, it would wound people, some would die immediately, some would be taken to the hospital and lose their life shortly after.

What happened next?

People's lives were so fragile and expendable; they'd be lost in a flash. Instead of mourning, death and dying became like a daily annoying chore we'd rather avoid, but we couldn't. We felt sad, but we had no time to feel or process things deeply. We had no space to mourn, because all we thought about was whether we would be next. Our survival instinct would take over our body, our mind, and we'd become numb, suppressing those feelings of grief, pushing them aside like a guest showing up at the door unannounced and unwanted. Because we had more important things to do than to mourn. We had to survive and keep going.

My first understanding of death came when I was six years old. My parents sent Amra and me to bed one night, and as we did when sleep didn't come quickly, we'd talk. That night, one of us mentioned that Grandmother was going to die someday. What that meant for us was that Grandmother would disappear forever, and she wouldn't be able to visit us anymore. But this was the case only for the grandmother, because she was old and she had gray hair, and she, according to us little children, was already one foot in a casket. By the time we realized Grandmother would forever be gone—and pretty soon no less—we began wailing so loudly that my mother stormed into our room, afraid that something must have happened to one of us.

"What is wrong, children?" She was known to panic fast. One of us broke the news.

"Grandmother will die someday." Tears were falling down our faces. Our mother stood there, looking like someone had buried her halfway in cement. She finally let out a nervous laugh.

"Hehe. She's not going to die. She is healthy and still young. Don't think like that." I could tell, even at that age, she felt disturbed. Not only had her children realized the meaning of mortality but she, too, was now reminded that death was inevitable even for healthy people. But our mother never told us that all of us would eventually go. She never said, *well, kids, that's the reality and we all have the same fate.* I had come to that realization on my own.

I looked at Matteo, numb and emotionless, taking the paper. There it was, a picture of Shel, bald and bearded, the familiar face that I recalled looking out into the distance, while giving me his advice on writing. I took one of his books that was sitting on the shelf of my desk, folded the paper in half, and put it inside the book before I put it back on the shelf. Part of me regretted not connecting with him again. After the war, I was still getting used to people dying of natural causes as opposed to by a bullet or shell shrapnel. I had not anticipated Shel's death, and why should I? People here seemed immortal next to those trying to survive a war.

Perhaps this was why I would think of death and dying frequently.

When I was a child, my religious maternal grandmother would often recite prayers in Arabic to Amra and me when we stayed overnight at her place. She would tuck us into bed in the room adjacent to hers, and then say the prayer for the evening, before sleep. The prayer never left my memory for some reason, but I never learned what it meant. She would also tell us what happened when a body died, according to the teachings of Islam. She'd say that when a body died, the soul would fly away and it would land elsewhere, in some other body, thus making the soul forever live, recycled in different bodies.

As a child it was easier to believe these stories. But during and after the war, I ceased to believe in life after death. With so many souls lost during the war, how many could be recycled in such a short time? Where would they all go? To what bodies would they fly and land upon? Weren't they too scared to stick around? Once, I decided that my soul wouldn't land anywhere after death, I developed a strange, disconcerting physical sensation in my body. Fear would wash over me each time I thought I would turn to ashes and never be able to use my faculties again as long as the vast universe existed.

We had a discussion in one of my writing classes where the main topic was death and dying. The instructor asked, "What precedes a good death?"

Silence in the room.

As if someone whispered in my ear, I raised my hand and said, "A good life."

The instructor got excited. "That's right!"

I was surprised at my own discovery. I tried not to think of death so often, pushing those thoughts aside, but also there were times when I didn't think my life had reached the requisite level of goodness. Sometimes I wondered, after witnessing sudden deaths during the war, after seeing what brutal things one human life can do to another, if life was as sacred as we made it out to be. Maybe death had its own charms.

I tried to think of things that could bring me joy and happiness. I was planning on visiting my family in Sarajevo soon. And that was enough for me to fill my soul with sparse cheer.

Shel's death was a rare moment when Matteo showed me any empathy.

On non-bad news days, I fought with Matteo all the time, like an angry teenager rebelling against her cold father. We lived in that apartment like roommates, or like a mouse and a cat, fighting for our territory. He resumed calling me names and more often than not I was "a stupid ignorant bitch" if I dropped something, said something, or did something to provoke his rage. He'd follow up with sincere apologies after the assaults.

I always felt he was more apologetic to himself for choosing the path of marrying me and getting stuck. He was on a roller-coaster—one minute mean and nasty, the next remorseful and apologetic—as if he was stuck in a vicious cycle. He seemed unhappy and unsettled, and he couldn't help but take that out on his worst enemy, his burden—me. He often reported he was having trouble at work and his boss often demanded projects of him he was unable to deliver. One time, he said he was supposed to give a presentation to a team of his colleagues, but when he stepped in front of the board, he became tongue-tied. He couldn't say a word. He didn't say a word. He blanked out and his presentation was over before it even started. All the new fancy custom-made suits he acquired for his job couldn't give him enough confidence to succeed. For this reason, I surmised, he couldn't be invested in my success either.

Once, I took Existentialism, a philosophy class that required deep analysis and thinking over a number of writing assignments. I came home one day and handed my paper to Matteo proudly to show off the A minus written in big red letters at the top of the first page. I entered his office, where he was typing on his computer. When I announced the good news, he lifted his arm, without turning around, signaling me to go away. Filled with rage, I crumbled the paper into a small ball and threw it at Matteo's direction, storming out of the office like a tsunami. I had no one to share my happiness with. My happiness was imaginary. My happiness was in the future. I was getting ready for a trip to Sarajevo, and the family reunion filled me with hope.

## ❧ 16 ❧

# MORE FEAR

**M**atteo converted two bedrooms into office spaces, one for him and one for me. He turned the third room into his bedroom, a sanctuary for him I was rarely allowed to visit. He had a comfortable bed and a TV set in his room. We put my old futon in his office, which doubled in the evening as my bedroom. The futon was uncomfortable and gave me horrible backaches. I'd wake up in the morning and feel the pain, then have to figure out how best to prop myself up and get out of bed. My other room compensated for the discomfort I felt at night. I enjoyed spending time there studying. Matteo made a huge desk in my office by placing two legs and a giant, ten-foot by three-foot tabletop on them. All of my studying took place at that desk. All the essays were written, problems solved, books read, research done, discoveries made—everything happened at that desk. Books became my new companions.

I signed up for a credit card one day so I could buy books and school supplies. Matteo paid for my classes, but he expected me to pay for my own books. When my first credit card bill showed up, I was surprised at how little I had to pay. How was it that I had bought hundreds of dollars of books and supplies but had to pay only twenty dollars? After a few months had passed, I noticed I owed the credit card company more than I had spent, and I finally realized—all on my own—that I was paying interest, and it was compounding on a monthly basis.

*Well, that's dumb!* I'd gotten trapped in a never-ending debt scheme. I was wasting my hard-earned money on paying a credit card company. I decided it was more sensible to pay off my entire credit card bill as soon as it arrived.

Through these kinds of trials and tribulations, I learned the system. Back in Bosnia, my parents could only have dreamed of having a credit card. They were trying to build their life together with the limited resources they had. To build their home back up, they took some furniture from the apartment we'd lived in during the war. Matteo was generous and he gave them cash every time we traveled to Sarajevo. Their monthly salary was minimal. With decades of experience, they still earned less than five hundred dollars a month, which barely got them by.

IN THE MID-WINTER OF 1999, MATTEO DECIDED TO TAKE ME to the mountains and get me on the ski slopes.

I grew up in a city surrounded by mountains. Because Sarajevo sat in a valley, the air inversion would often form smog in the city and, on some winter days, you could barely see your own fingers in front of you. On such days, Jasmina and I, still teenagers, would go outside and light a cigarette in the middle of the street and walk around, amused that we couldn't be seen. To escape the smog and bad air quality, we'd often take family day trips to a nearby mountain, either Igman or Trebević, and spend a few hours walking in the woods, looking for tiny forest strawberries. On our way up, we'd watch the clouds rest on the city like foam sitting in a huge coffee cup. In the winter, we'd bring sleds and hit the hills, trying to avoid other people on sleds, or skiers on the trails. I'd wake up every single morning, looking at the Sarajevo

Butmir International Airport and Mount Igman in the background. The deep green beauty of the forest brought me peace and comfort. In 1984, Sarajevo held the Winter Olympic Games, and those mountains were filled with tourists. We rented our apartment to a couple of Croats from Zagreb who came to Sarajevo with the Olympic Games committee, while we stayed with my grandmother in the Old Town. When we returned home, we discovered a helium balloon in Amra's and my room. Eventually, we also discovered they had taped over a snippet of a radio program we had on an audio cassette. A song of Hanka Paldum, a folk singer, would play and suddenly be interrupted by man's voice. Amra and I laughed at this discovery.

Amra and I never learned how to ski, despite our easy access to the mountains. One year, my father retrieved a pair of skis and boots from a recycling place, but none of us had a clue that skis and boots had to be customfitted. He put them in the basement, hoping either Amra or I would take interest one day and decide to hit the slopes. But that never happened.

I didn't know if Matteo felt bad for me or for himself, but for some reason he decided to take me to the mountains and get me ski lessons. A few days prior, we went to a sporting goods store and bought ski gear. We woke up early Saturday morning, got in the car, and headed north on Route 93 to New Hampshire. Matteo's brother Fabio had been teaching skiing at Cannon Mountain for years already. He'd established himself there and viewed the mountain as his second home. He rented a motel room near the mountain for the whole season. During the day, he gave ski lessons to beginners or more experienced skiers, and at night, several ski instructors would get together and go out for dinner at a local restaurant.

As we drove, the valleys and fields bloomed into hills, getting increasingly whiter as we drove closer to Cannon Mountain, until the most majestic views appeared in front of my eyes. The different shapes, colors, and slopes of the White Mountains took my breath away and for a second, I felt at home. I belonged there. The view looked like a Renaissance painting on a museum wall, and I could see myself standing in front of it and staring at it for a long time. As we approached the mountain, Matteo told me to look to my left and I'd see the Old Man on the Mountain.

"What's the Old Man?" I asked, confused.

"It's a rock shaped like a man's profile." I looked up, and there it was, the face of an old man at the top of a mountain, standing there and looking over the valley, over the small lake between trees, and the highway that eventually turned into a one-way lane in each direction. Within seconds, the view of the Old Man disappeared and from the new angle, the man turned into a random rock.

Years later, the Old Man collapsed and so did his admirers' joy. It was a sad day when the Old Man died.

CANNON MOUNTAIN, SEEN FROM THE HIGHWAY, SEEMED STEEP and enthralling, and those white slopes were soon to be a place I'd frequent. To learn skiing, I started on the bunny slopes, making the infamous pizza wedge until I became more proficient. Soon after, I'd accompany Matteo every weekend, each time trying to perfect my skiing by either taking lessons or skiing alone on the slopes.

One weekend, Matteo suggested I drive. "You need more experience driving on the highway. Why don't we go ahead and take your car?"

When we crossed the New Hampshire border, the highway ahead of us opened up like a flower; it was beautiful and wide, and I lost track of how fast I was going, which turned out to be well over eighty miles per hour. Out of nowhere, blue lights flashed behind me. As a police car caught up to me, Matteo said, "Pull over, pull over."

I switched into panic mode. "How?"

"Put your right blinker on and move all the way to the right lane until you can pull over onto the shoulder."

I hoped I was dreaming. Maybe the police car wasn't chasing *me*.

I was terrified of authorities with guns. Ever since I'd arrived in the United States, I'd had two distinct recurring dreams. In one dream, Serbs occupied our neighborhood as my family and I hid, waiting for them to come and execute us on the spot, like they had killed our neighbors during the war. In another dream, the war was just starting, and I was planning on committing suicide before the Serbs came for us. Those dreams were vivid and real, and I'd wake up terrified and sweating, nonetheless relieved I'd only been dreaming.

But the police car following us wasn't a dream. I finally pulled over into the shoulder, and the police car parked right behind me.

"Get your ID ready." Matteo said as he was looking for registration information in the glove compartment.

I opened up my window, and the police lady showed up on my side.

"Good morning. Do you know why I pulled you over, ma'am?" I was shaking, unable to utter a word. I closed my hands to conceal the trembling. My fear was so grand that my mind blanked and my ability to speak tanked.

Matteo intervened. He sounded calm.

"Officer, my wife here... she's a new driver." I looked at the wheel ahead of me, thinking of ways to perhaps escape, push on the gas pedal and disappear into the mountains. "Did she drive too fast or something?"

"Sir, she was driving well over the speed limit. The speed limit in New Hampshire is sixty-five miles per hour. Your wife was driving over eighty. Can I see your license and registration?" I handed her the paperwork, and she walked back to her car.

Minutes passed, and silence filled the car. I had obviously lost sense of how fast I was driving. The highway seemed to have sloped downwards and gravity had sped us up. Minutes passed like years, enough time to create a scene in my mind. I imagined the lady officer coming back to my car, putting a gun to my temple and threatening my life. That she'd then pull the trigger and my numb brain would fly all over the car. I dreaded what was to come next.

She walked back to the car and handed back my license and registration.

"I'm going to give you a warning this time. Next time, I can't say you won't get a ticket. Have a good day, folks, and drive safe." She smiled and walked away.

I woke up from this terrible nightmare. I sat there for a little while, or until the police car disappeared. I pushed the gas pedal and my car began to move towards the grand mountains, my happy place.

The memory of this event stayed with me, alive and vivid. As trauma survivors, we either motivate ourselves to forget fast, or the traumatic event stays with us like a scar. Our memory becomes selective. Trauma puts us in survival mode, based on fear, void of happy thoughts. After the incident, I drove most carefully, sitting on the edge of my seat, anticipating the blue flashing light behind me at any moment. I felt fear slowly seep in, making up stories in my head. I found no way to cope but to give into this fear. It was exhausting. Fear is exhausting. And before we know it, it drives us to escape, to do something uncanny, something that others perhaps wouldn't fully understand, in order to survive.

# 17

## JOB HOPPING

I wanted to shake off my fears, my pain. I wanted to live a happy life, without quirks, fears, cracks. I wanted to form strong friendships and feel close to people. I wished to belong in a place where I felt safe and comfortable, without fearing that safety and comfort might disappear quickly.

But instead, I ran.

The prep room no longer seemed to work for me. Al would constantly whistle, and I would lose my mind every time he began producing these symphonies. I couldn't concentrate on my work, and when our clients came over to schedule an AV equipment, I had to ask them to spell their names over and over again, which they'd patiently do on hearing my foreign accent.

I walked into the prep room one day and went to look for José to let him know I was quitting. During the same time, Claudia told me her department in a healthcare unit was looking for someone to make calls and confirm doctor's appointments for next-day sessions. I showed up in my new car every day, and Claudia would give me a list of patients, their names and phone numbers, and I'd go down the list until I was done. There would be about twenty patients per day, and sometimes they'd pick up the phone, and sometimes I'd have to leave a voicemail message.

On the second day, I called my first patient, and when a woman answered the phone, I asked for her by name and she immediately became enraged. When I told her about her appointment, she hung up the phone immediately without letting me say goodbye. Distressed about the whole episode, I ran to Claudia.

"Some woman just hung on me, and I don't know why."

"How so?" Claudia was surprised to hear this. She'd never had a problem with her staff confirming appointments before.

"Well, I asked for her by name, then I told her she had an appointment tomorrow, and then she hung up on me."

"How did you say it?" Claudia put her manager hat on.

"She answered the phone, and I simply asked if Mrs *Peen-elope* was there." Claudia burst out laughing. I stood there, looking at her without the slightest clue as to why she was laughing. She tried to speak, but she was failing, and she'd burst out laughing every time she tried to say something.

"You said..." she laughed again, "you said what?"

"I said, 'is Mrs *Peen-elope* there'?"

Claudia busted out another laugh. She wiped the tears on her eyes, and then she said, "That's not how you pronounce her name. It's *Pe-ne-lo-pee.*"

I had apparently offended this woman by my immigrant ignorance. But I understood her. People had a hard time pronouncing my name, and for the longest time, before they could say it, I'd teach them: it's *Na-DEE-ya*. They'd finally get it with trial and error.

The job of confirming doctor's appointments didn't make me happy. In fact, it made me feel inadequate, awkward, and miserable, especially after the Peen-elope episode. I hated talking on the phone. In my first few months of living in Boston, every time I went to leave a message, I wrote down everything I was going to say on a piece of paper, from "hello" to "talk to you later." If a person didn't answer their phone, I'd leave a voicemail message by reading the note and breathing heavily from the fear and anxiety of leaving an empty monologue that was to be heard at a later time. The recipient would probably have picked up my fear and I rarely received a return call.

After two weeks of confirming appointments, I walked into Claudia's office and told her I was quitting. I wrote her a heart-felt thank you note and put it in an A4 white envelope. When I handed it to her, she didn't show any emotion, as if she had experienced her staff quitting many times before.

I hustled looking for another job. With the economy booming, I had no trouble landing one quickly. I read an advertisement in the newspaper one day that Re/Max First Reality in Newton Center was looking for a receptionist. The following day, I drove to the office and asked to fill out the job application. I met Stephanie, the office manager, a friendly young woman with curly hair, and glasses covering her blue eyes. She had a high-pitched voice when she came out to greet me, and she took my filled out job application informing me she'd take a look at it and call me back if interested.

The following day, I came home from an errand and had a voicemail message from Stephanie. I called her back to arrange the interviews, and when she answered, she said, "I love your voicemail message. I was laughing all alone in my office." I'd tried to have fun with it. Voicemail service did not exist in Bosnia.

*Hi, you have reached Nadija. I am either on the other line or I am vacuuming and I can't hear the phone ring. Please leave me a voicemail message, and I will get back to you as soon as I can.*

"We'd love for you to come to our office and meet a few people," she declared. "How about tomorrow?"

I got the job and learned it quickly, mainly how real estate agents operated. They were like sharks in an open water, looking for any sale opportunity. They seemed competitive amongst themselves, and the office had come up with a system of tracking cold calls and assigning each agent to those customers.

A board with the names of each agent hung on the wall, and

there was a colored dot indicating what agent would get the next cold call. As part of the training, Stephanie instructed me not to give any information about a property on the market that a customer might inquire about. I had to transfer their call promptly to the listing agent so they could discuss their customers' needs directly.

One time, on a Saturday, when most agents were visiting open houses and busy running around, I received a call about a house that had just come onto the market.

"I need to speak to the listing agent," the customer demanded.

"I'm sorry, but the agent is unavailable right now. May I transfer your call to him?" I offered politely.

"I just need to know the square footage. Can you just tell me the square footage of the house?"

"I'm sorry, sir, but you need to speak with the agent directly. I can transfer you to him now."

"Drop dead!" He hung up the phone.

I couldn't stand this uncalled for viciousness. Sure, the man didn't want me dead, per se, but hearing those words triggered me into believing he did. I slowly put the phone receiver down and clenched my teeth, trying not to cry. Many years later, I'd learn to ignore mean people like him (it's them, not you—people would say), but back home in Bosnia, my neighbors wanted me dead for no rhyme or reason. I was a target of sport killing, like the recreational hunting of animals. The man's voice, unknown and distant, brought me close to the war days I still frequented in my nightmares and desperately wanted to escape. The phrase *Drop Dead* was random, but so was my neighbor's desire to kill me.

A short time later, a worse incident occurred, where I found myself in a copy machine room, getting new listings printed to update the listing catalogue displayed on the table in the office foyer. David, a tall, fit man, an agent who had been there for years, approached me and put his hand on my buttocks, saying,

"Thank you for your help earlier. I really appreciate it." As he spoke, he wiggled his resting hand a bit and my whole body shook. He quickly left the room and disappeared.

I stood there in disbelief that he had violated my space with what was clearly sexual harassment. When I came home, I told Matteo about it, but he didn't seem alarmed or upset. He suggested I write a letter explaining what had happened to the agency owner, Alan. When my brother-in-law Fabio heard what happened, he offered his opinion.

"You know, you could be driving a Mercedes like them." He was suggesting if I took them to court, they'd pay through the roof. But I had no such inclination, nor did I have anyone to support me if I chose to pursue it. Instead, I wrote a letter and left it in Alan's mailbox. I expected him to call me to his office, given the seriousness of the situation, and to offer some kind of reparation for David's bad deed.

To my surprise, next time Alan saw me, which was in the back hallway, he stopped me and said, "I got your letter and I read it. And I guarantee it will not happen again. I spoke with David and he apologized. He confirmed it would never happen again. Okay?"

"Okay."

"Okay." He repeated.

I kept staring at his white head as he spoke to me. It didn't seem clear how old Alan was. His white hair made me think he had aged and was well into his seventies or eighties but his energy and fierceness indicated otherwise. Once, he asked me to draft a letter to a client for him and he instructed me to write only the word, "No", on a single sheet of paper.

"Anything else?" I'd asked.

"That's it. But make it bigger." I increased the font size to eighteen and as he stood behind and watched me, he'd repeat. "Bigger."

I increased the size yet again, and he repeated his instruction until the word "No" filled the entire page. I turned around, and his face was red, filled with anger and revenge.

Every day I walked into the agency, I couldn't help but see evil, ugly shadows dancing around and following me like dangerous beasts. I became uneasy about how David had treated me and even more so with how Alan chose to respond. In my mind, it was wrong, but I couldn't do anything about it. After a year and a half, I resolved to seek a job elsewhere. A few weeks after the incident, I walked into Stephanie's office to give her my notice. She was genuinely surprised and disappointed.

"We will miss you." They bought a cake for me and invited anyone who was around to stop by and wish me farewell. Alan's wife Janet pulled a box from her purse and handed it to me. Inside was a pair of golden earring hoops that almost made me change my perception of the place. But no. Those scary shadows were still peeking from the corners, and I never wanted to see them again.

The following week, I started a new job at Harvard University where I was already taking classes. I hoped it would finally be a place where I could grow and belong.

## ❧ 18 ❧

# VISITING "HOME"

I landed at Sarajevo International airport in the evening, when Mount Igman turned into a big dark mass. I couldn't see its evergreen tree forests that I used to see clearly from my old room when I focused hard enough in the daytime. I stepped outside the plane onto a small runway, with the Tunnel of Hope underneath connecting what used to be the site of the siege of Sarajevo and the neighborhood across the airport called Hrasnica. The tunnel was built by the Bosnian Army sometime in 1993, and would become the only hope of bringing in food and supplies to desperate and hungry Sarajevans.

On my way out, I saw a familiar face, an acquaintance I had spent time with along with a few mutual friends during the war. I waved to him, happy to see someone familiar right away and feel at home. But when I rested my eyes on him a little longer, I read his lips: *Go fuck yourself.* If I deserved that, I didn't know why.

When I came out of the terminal, my entire family was waiting to greet me. Only then did I notice how spent and Bosnian they looked, with their decaying teeth in their smiling faces, and eyes deeply set in their sockets, their skinny bodies shaped from the constant hunger during the war. We awkwardly hugged, not the tight embrace signaling happiness and joy at our reunion. Dženana stood behind her mother's legs and looked at me shyly, perhaps wondering if that was really me, her aunt, coming from so far away. An aunt who showed up once a year, confused about her own identity and belonging.

Back in Boston, I rarely talked to my parents. Overseas calls were expensive and landline calls were at almost a dollar a minute. With my meager salary, I could scarcely afford it. Our correspondence consisted of letters summarizing our lives on a few pages. On the rare occasions we did talk, I didn't have much to stay. I'd stutter, forgetting the Bosnian words to express myself freely. I didn't dare tell them about my frequent fights with Matteo, or how my life with him as a roommate had become nearly unbearable, and that I had no other place to go. That I was lost, I had no friends, no one to look out for me or give me advice. I wanted my parents to think my new home was filled with peace and harmony, that I was succeeding in all areas of life. I reported on small victories, anything from learning how to drive to learning how to ski. And most importantly, that school was going well and that I was getting satisfactory grades.

But it wasn't always me being awkward in those phone calls. My paternal grandmother surprised me by calling one day while I was sitting at my desk studying. I picked up the phone, and on the other line, I heard a familiar, sweet quiet voice.

"Nadija, it's Grandmother. What's new?"

I told her all about school, the weather, my life in a nutshell. She was silent for a second, then said, "What else is new?"

"Mmmm. Not much really. I am going to school and work every day, you know, I keep busy."

"A-ha." Silence. "What else is new?" I nervously began laughing, hoping the call would wrap up as soon as possible. I excused myself, feeling helpless. Grandmother wasn't as sharp anymore. As long as I'd known her, she'd always been quiet and sweet, but this conversation took it to a different level. In my uneasiness, I had to flee. I hoped our interactions in person would be better.

But I had no luck seeing my grandmother on my next trip or ever again. She passed a few months after our phone conversation, and I received a letter from my dad, telling me about his mother's death.

*Dear Dikili,*

*The most significant event is the death of my mother at age eighty. She was quite ill the last ten days of her life, but she didn't suffer for too long. Death of a mother is the biggest loss for every man. What can you do? That's life—interwoven by sad and joyful events.*

When I read it, I felt numb and emotionless. Numbness and a lack of emotion became my new reality. I hung onto memories of my grandmother and remembered her as a sweet, quiet lady who'd had a tough life.

MY PARENTS' BUILDING STOOD RIGHT ACROSS FROM THE airport, one street separating the two. Even though it was less than a ten-minute walk home, my father drove to the airport to pick me up in his new car. It was an old and used Opel Kadet, which didn't rival the brand-new Škoda he'd bought one year before the war. It looked like it belonged to an earlier era. We all packed into the tiny car and rode across the street.

It had been almost a year since my parents had moved back to their old house. Right after the war, our neighborhood had been handed to the European humanitarian companies to rebuild the buildings and make them habitable, so people could return to their homes. The building my parents lived in had been nicely restored and looked like it had done before the war, but in different colors. But not all of the neighborhood had been rebuilt. Some buildings were still only rubble, as if someone decided to keep it that way as a monument. I surmised it would take much longer to restore the parts that had been decimated, like an avocado or banana smashed in a bowl that could never be put back into its original form. Some of our neighbors returned, and many didn't. Our street looked like a ghost town, starkly different from the lively place bustling with children playing their favorite games before the war. Not long ago, Serbs walked on these streets, for the first time on June 17, 1992 when they occupied the neighborhood. They killed seventy-four people that day, making the neighborhood a literal ghost town.

Even if those ghosts lingered in the air, my parents couldn't care less, because they were thrilled to be back in their "own space" despite it not looking like its former self.

When we entered the apartment, I was surprised to see how it had been transformed back into its old self. Instead of the naked cement we'd found upon returning in 1996, the floors were covered with high-quality wood, quite an improvement on the worn-out parquet from before the war. The windows and kitchen cabinets were new. Amra's and my old room seemed a lot smaller than I recalled. My parents had amassed furniture from different places and it looked a bit bulkier in the small space.

I noticed the wallpaper was missing, replaced with fresh green paint in both rooms. The wallpaper before the war had been white and textured like corduroy material, getting dirty in the winter from the smoke coming from the wood stove in the kitchen. My parents had used the wood stove to save money on electricity bills. They'd buy a ton of coal and chopped wood and keep it down in our basement space. Every day, my dad would go two stories down with a bucket, fill it with coal and wood and use it to supply the kitchen. The stove seemed heavy and the top was made of iron, with a door in the front and a circle on the top in the middle you could lift to put more coal inside. My mom would grab a long iron fork every once in a while, and stir the burning coal so the fire wouldn't die out.

The stove produced heavy smoke, contributing to the winter smog outside, but it also made our corduroy wallpaper dark. My parents would grab another bucket in the spring, fill it with warm water and detergent, dip a sponge in the water and remove the dirt from the walls. In the summer, since the stove was deemed useless, my mom would cover it and the top looked as white as snow. She'd place a piece of crochet-work on top, like pretty much everything she had covered around the house.

Like everything else, the stove had been taken. When I think of all the things stolen from us, my sorrow does not start or end with the stove. I was more attached to sentimental items we built and collected before the war, such as our photos. Since we did not find any photos upon our return home, except for a random one in the front hedges, I don't know what I looked like as a baby. The baby photos of me had faded in my memory. Was I plump? Did I crack frequent smiles? Was my hair dark, blonde, some other color? Did I resemble my father or my mother? As long as I live, I will never find out.

SHORTLY AFTER I ARRIVED, THE BUZZER DOWNSTAIRS RANG. Ever since my parents and some of our old neighbors had returned, the front door was locked day and night to prevent people freely walking in. We never had to do that before the war. In fact, the front door was always wide open with people coming in and going out all the time. When I was a child, gypsies often walked into our building and went door-to-door begging for money. The craftier ones would knock on our doors and ask if we had an umbrella to be fixed. My mother would tell us to look through the peep hole whenever someone rang the doorbell. One time, I got tricked into believing I heard our next-door neighbor's voice, but when I opened the door, a short gypsy woman holding her baby stood there, with her palm extended asking for money. I was so scared by the surprise that I slammed the door.

When gypsies weren't asking for money, they took dancing bears on the streets and gathered people around the bear placing his front paws in the air and moving to the drum beat. Those brown bears, ones we only saw in a mountain forest, seemed tamed and tranquil. As a child, I'd picture one storming into the audience and attacking. But it never happened. This tradition never struck me as strange until years passed and the memory crossed my mind. Not in a million years would I ever see a dancing bear on the streets of the United States. And never again in post-war Sarajevo.

While gypsies no longer frequented our neighborhood, our neighbors now took extra precautions.

"You never know who might just storm in and come steal our stuff. Better safe than sorry." A neighbor said. The war fears flew around like ghosts.

My friend Melina and my mom's colleague Blaženka arrived at the same time and fought over the small space in the hallway to take off their shoes. A surprise! What were they doing here?

My mother brought in plates of food from the kitchen to the living room and placed them on the table they had taken from the apartment we lived in during the war. Amra put music on, and soon the gathering turned into a rowdy party. Cigarette smoke filled the room and Dženana, the small child sitting on the corner of the sofa, looked a bit puzzled. I watched that beautiful small face through the deadly cloud. I was jet-legged, feeling like I had been drinking alcohol all night, and didn't feel like partaking in the celebration. What were we celebrating exactly? Was the party an attempt to restore happiness and joy for all the years lost during the war? I couldn't recall seeing them so joyful, so I thought of the possibility that my parents had simply lost their minds.

Eventually, they all stood up and hugged each other, singing in unison while I sat on the couch, bewildered by the entire scene. Anis was standing in a corner of the room, taking pictures like it was a wedding ceremony.

I began to resent my family's ignorance. Didn't they know what it was like to travel for fourteen hours? Did they not know that second-hand cigarette smoke could kill? And most importantly, didn't they care?

A couple of days after my arrival in Sarajevo, my arch enemy, asthma, returned. When I moved to Boston, it had nearly disappeared. My lungs must have appreciated the moisture in the air coming off the Atlantic Ocean. The asthma attacks dwindled soon after, and I no longer woke in the middle of the night or early morning, trying to catch a breath. I had learned over time that my visits to Bosnia required bringing an inhaler or two for when the enemy struck.

Soon I also learned that asthma could be provoked by intense stress, so I began to think that being in Sarajevo triggered the attacks. Wherever I went, the aftermath of the war appeared before me, reminding me of the intense suffering we'd experienced in the siege. With those scenes confronting me, all too real and unavoidable, it was difficult to move on from the past. Some said time would heal. But for Bosnia and Sarajevo, time stood still. The rubble and suffering were still present and persistent.

I spent a lot of time in my old room. My mother, who spent all her time in the living room, had hung a clock on the wall, and I hated the ticking noise. It sounded as if someone was beating me over the head with a bat. I tried to ignore it, but my focus was only on the clock even when there was other commotion in the room. I'd run to my room and close myself in there, reading books, spending time alone, perhaps waiting for someone to knock on the door to check up on me. But no one ever did.

The previous time I visited, my mother tried to kiss me as I was resting on the couch, but I jerked my head and made the face, *leave me alone*. In the loneliness I'd become accustomed to, I'd forgotten how to say *I love you, I miss you, I wish you were here*. There was something about feeling vulnerable that meant it could break me or her, and I wanted to avoid further breakage at all costs. My mom eventually learned to leave me alone.

I'd resurface and venture to the living room only to preach

what I had learned in the United States. My mother's teeth had started to decay during the war, when going to a dentist was only a dream. I'd get angry and begin, "You really need to fix your teeth. Look at all those cavities. They're all black for Pete's sake, why don't you go see a dentist?"

Her gums looked like they were filled with water, all swollen and protruding from her mouth. In my new surroundings, I had learned to go for teeth cleaning twice a year, for a dentist check-up once a year, and to floss my teeth at home in between.

"I'm afraid I didn't ask you for your advice." She'd say.

"Well, go ahead, lose all your teeth, I don't give a shit. But you will regret it." My mom would listen and pretend she wasn't paying attention to me. She'd inhale cigarette smoke and quickly exhale while shrugging her shoulders and her face would get lost in the smoke. To this day, she had not learned how to properly smoke.

"Seriously? So, you're going to smoke permanently now? The war is over, why are you still smoking?"

"It relaxes me." She said. She'd blink—one, two, three times —like she was getting uncomfortable or nervous about our exchange.

"But you don't know how to smoke. You just exhale it as soon as you inhale it. That's even worse. You can get mouth cancer, like Freud did." I was on a roll. She shrugged her shoulders again. She didn't want to hear the ranting of the wisdom I had apparently acquired in my new home.

What was happening to me? Was I turning into Matteo who'd deemed me an ignorant bitch and wanted to teach me lessons every time I messed up? Did my mother feel abused by my constant complaints about her unhealthy behaviors? She wanted to be left in peace. Now was not the time for someone who had escaped to greener pastures to try to improve her life. It took me a while to understand why no one cared to visit me in the room while I was alone for hours at a time. I was slowly exhibiting behaviors of nagging and constantly preaching, to eradicate ignorance that I myself hated. I intended to make my mother's life better, but I came across as critical and a know-it-all.

When the day came for me to leave, we all felt lighter. Or, perhaps, only I did. I realized I could just as easily spend time alone in my room in Nonentum while avoiding an asthma attack. On that trip, I flew Air Italia via Rome to Boston, and my airplane didn't depart from Rome until the following day. Because I was still traveling with my Bosnian passport that would get me into only a handful countries without a visa, I got stuck at the airport for the night. I walked around the airport forever, looking through the store windows and seeing all kinds of items I couldn't afford. The stores were beginning to close for the night, and shortly after, the whole airport died out. Only a few passengers, unlucky like me, stuck around with nowhere to go.

I found a lonesome corner with a few chairs adjacent to one another and I planted my backpack on one of them, forming a makeshift bed for the night. I took out the inhaler from the front pocket of my backpack, released a couple of puffs into my mouth, and lay down on my bed, reflecting on my recent trip to Sarajevo.

I had yet to feel at home anywhere. Somewhere, someday.

# "NADIJA'S STREET"

M atteo told me we'd been invited to an outdoor party at his friend Bob's, who lived in an old house with a small front yard a few blocks from Harvard Square.

Matteo knew Bob from growing up in Newton. He told me Bob came from a Jewish family and now he lived in the Cambridge house he'd inherited from his parents. He hadn't worked for many years and took advantage of his comfortable inheritance by visiting cafés all day long and sipping coffee while reading books.

When we arrived at Bob's, a short man with gray hair and a hat greeted us. Bob was a friendly man, always ready with a smile that made his eyes squint. Later, I learned he knew all there was to know about jazz. His house, which had dated furniture and unappealing cracked walls and old wallpaper, had a small living room. In it was an old chair sitting next to wall-to-wall shelves where he'd tucked his precious vinyl records. He was proud of his collection. In a conversation about music, he'd go to a shelf and pull out the vinyl without thinking twice about its location and then proceed to tell an involved story about the artist, the music, the songs—too much information to take in at one time. He also wrote poems and, later, I'd often offer my stories for him to read and give me feedback on. We'd go to a local café and, while sipping coffee, Bob would read my work, look up at me once in a while to offer a smile, and look down again to keep reading. He'd burst out laughing and then apologize. He said my English was difficult to correct without obliterating the meaning of my words. We became friends.

At the party, I was quiet as usual, observing small pods of people gathering, having beers, and talking among themselves. I never understood how it could be called a party. I was used to Bosnian parties, where everyone would sit in a circle, sing, play guitar, drink, laugh, feel united. This wasn't a party in comparison. It was a gathering where people were segregated and lonely. If you were shy and never learned how to mingle with people you barely knew, this party would not be for you.

I was standing all alone when Bob approached me.

"So, I hear you're from Bosnia originally."

"Yeah."

"I have a friend who went there a year ago. She loved it. Her name is Sara. You guys need to meet up."

I had already heard about Sara. When she went to visit Bosnia and Croatia the year after I moved to the United States, she ended up going to an island in the Adriatic Sea where she met my friends Vedran, Robert, and Gordan. The three brothers went to the island for a drumming workshop. Sara and Vedran hooked up and dated during her visit. Vedran often mentioned my name; he told her I lived in Boston and she should look me up when she returned.

Sara was a daughter of a woman, Ellen, who, according to Bob, was one of the Mayflower descendants. Bob and Ellen went to high school together and had known each other since. Ellen also lived in Cambridge while she taught Bosnian and Serbo-Croatian at Harvard. When she was young, destiny found her in the former Yugoslavia where she studied and began to speak the language fluently. She'd married a man there, and together they ended up having two daughters, Sara and Rachel. When Sara turned twelve, they decided to move back to the United States where they would raise their children.

"I'd love to meet Sara." I told Bob, but I was skeptical since I had not had any luck meeting any former Yugoslavs I could befriend.

My opportunity to meet Sara didn't come until Bob invited me to an art performance at Zeitgeist, a small gallery located on Hampshire Street in Cambridge. It had been months since there'd been any mention of Sara. Neither of us had bothered to reach out to the other.

ZEITGEIST WAS AN OPEN SPACE, AROUND A THOUSAND SQUARE feet, decorated by rows of chairs and a small stage at the back. The space could easily be converted to a music performance stage or a gallery. Among the rows of chairs, I sat alone at the back, trying to interpret the performance with my limited knowledge of jazz. I showed up because it would give me a chance to do something other than sit between the four walls of my lonely home office.

When the performance ended, Bob came up to me and brought a youngish looking girl with blue eyes and light brown hair. She extended her arm and said, "Hi, I'm Sara."

"You're Sara? Sara! Sara Novak!" We both began to laugh and gave each other an instant hug like we had known each other our whole lives, but been separated at some point.

Sara quickly became my best friend; someone who spoke my language. We'd go places, her mom would invite me over for dinner, we would think of projects to get involved with to busy ourselves. Unlike me, Sara was cheerful, adventurous, a magnet to the people she met.

She called me up one day to ask me if I could participate in an installation event taking place at the Harvard Graduate School of Education, Gutman Library, for a local artist of

Yugoslav descent. She'd announce the installation pieces in English, and I'd follow by announcing in Bosnian. I'd just be reading from a piece of paper, but I got nervous just thinking that all ears and eyes would be on me, even for only a few seconds.

When the time came, Sara spoke loudly and clearly without any reservation or fear. Then I followed, opening my mouth, struggling to enunciate my words and hide my braces, afraid that someone would laugh at me. Matteo, who came along, later told me I could have done a better job.

"I couldn't really hear you well, and I don't know if people could understand you." He had no reservations about giving me constructive criticism.

Whether I failed or not, it didn't stop Sara from coming up with another idea. She told me that Zeitgeist would let her have a photography show where she'd display her black and white photographs taken in Sarajevo. I came over to her place to check out the photos, and she excitedly told me that the date had already been chosen and she was about to print invitations and fliers to advertise the event. She took me to her bedroom where the framed photographs were waiting to be hung on the Zeitgeist wall. As I looked closer, I saw one particular photo in which the scenery looked awfully familiar.

"Wait, you took this one?"

"Of course." Sara said, surprised I'd even asked.

"Sara, this is my street. You took a photo of my street."

"No way!" She couldn't contain herself.

The photo was taken at a fork on my street, where one side led to another neighborhood and the other to a local supermarket. When I was a child, I'd take daily trips to this supermarket to buy fresh bread, so Amra and I could have breakfast before school. At the beginning of the war, the neighbors smashed all the windows and looted the entire place. In the photo was a building with numerous holes pierced by bullets and shrapnel and in front of it stood a tree. It was a surprise the tree had survived. Most trees during the war were cut for fuel to heat homes. When Sara took that photo near the fork, my building stood behind her, and she never dreamed she'd meet someone who had walked those streets and lived in that building.

"Wow! This is crazy, don't you think?" After some thought, she came back to me and added, "I think I'm going to name it *Nadija's Street.*" Before the event, she reframed the photo, adding the new name in pencil.

I TOLD SARA THAT I WAS WRITING WAR STORIES. I TOOK AN Introduction to Memoir class after I realized that psychology classes didn't give me any of the psychological relief I'd hoped for. Instead, I had learned too many psychology theories that I couldn't memorize, and written papers on stimulus and conditioning, behaviorism, observing young children. I decided that psychology wasn't for me after all.

For my memoir class, my instructor, Jane Brox, an established author of memoirs about farm life, gave all students a chance to read in front of class and have their pieces critiqued. My turn came and I began to read. The story was about my family learning that the enemy had taken over our neighborhood, and how my father consoled my mother that everything would be all right. I'd named the story *Everything Will Be Alright, Darling.* When I finished reading, tears flowed down my face. One could hear a pin drop for seconds to come. People's faces looked either sad or bewildered; everyone was speechless.

Jane finally broke the silence:

"That must have been really hard." she said. Just looking at her, you could see her empathy and unbridled goodness. She ended up giving me an A at the end of the semester.

Sara came to me and asked, "Do you want to read a story at my event?"

"Are you sure?" With my anxiety and never-ending criticism

echoing in the back of my mind, I could see a disaster looming at the event.

*Stupid ignorant bitch.*

"I mean, I don't really have any experience reading in front of a large audience."

That wasn't entirely true. When I was a child, in grades one through three, I often recited poems in front of the entire school during the Yugoslav national holidays. The school choir sang patriotic songs, and in between them, children came on stage and recited poetry. I'd take days to memorize mine and would practice them aloud or in my mind until I didn't have to think about it, until it could just flow out of my mouth intact, freely. I wore a blue hat with a red star on it, a white shirt, blue skirt, and a red bandana over my neck to symbolize pride in red, blue, and white, the colors of the Yugoslavia flag. That's all we knew. The children growing up in the former Yugoslavia were called *pioniri* (pioneers), further promulgating the socialist ideas that Tito had installed in all of us. *Bratstvo i jedinstvo*—brotherhood and unity, the country's motto. After his death, even after the war, Tito was greatly missed. People felt nostalgia for the days he was still alive-he was like a caring grandfather making sure all his children and grandchildren got along well. People held onto the memory of him like an amulet.

On one such recital occasion, the children came out, one by one, and recited sections of the poem named P.I.O.N.I.R. I was a P and came out first: *Ponosna sam. Proud I am,* was the beginning of my lines. I had no fear of speaking in public. In fact, I was so good at it my teacher gave me other assignments and had me speak in front of the entire school. My parents would sit somewhere in the audience, but my eyes would rest on the far wall in front of me and I would focus on my lines.

"You don't need much experience. All you need to do is read from a piece of paper. If you want, you can practice in front of me." Sara's energy rubbed off on me. Whatever she touched was bound to succeed.

"Okay, I will do it."

"Great! You'll be great, you'll see."

The day came, and when I showed up at Zeitgeist, Sara was already there, running around, making sure everything was all set and in perfect order. I came to a table in a corner where bottles of wine and empty glasses stood. Next to them were invitations. I picked one up, and noticed she'd included my name:

*Nadija Damiani*
*Reading from her war memoir*

My palms began to sweat and my heart beat fast. I grabbed a bottle of wine and poured myself a glass, hoping it would calm my nerves.

A crowd began to thicken and Sara disappeared into her tasks. I sat on a chair and waited for my turn. Half an hour into the show, Sara came up front and thanked everyone who'd come to see her photographs. Her voice sounded confident, filled with pride and assurance. By then, the wine had somewhat calmed me and I was ready to perform. She announced my name, and I went up front to sit on a high chair and began to read.

The room was silent. Just like in my memoir class, I could hear people breathing and the occasional cough. I anticipated that people would start to laugh at me at any moment, and I'd run through the door as fast as possible and never write another word again.

As I read, I asked myself, *why am I doing this? Does anyone really care? Why would they?* I tried to hush these thoughts, in fear that they would stop me from reading and that would be the end of it. I'd embarrass Sara and she would never speak to me again. I did not want to disappoint her. I kept going. My voice sounded like a rollercoaster as my thoughts ebbed and flowed. At one point, I sounded bold, and at others, my voice would be quiet. I tried not to think of the people sitting and listening. I was all alone, and that thought comforted me.

And then it ended. I kept my eyes down, embarrassed about what I had just shared. A few seconds passed, and what did I see from the corner of my eye? A standing ovation. I kept my head down and walked off the stage.

The following day, I heard from Sara. "Thank you for reading your memoir. That was really great."

I was glad that Sara was satisfied with the event, but I felt spent. I'd let myself be vulnerable and exposed, showing the irreparable damage made by the war to so many people. "Listen, I have something for you. Maybe we can get together tomorrow?"

"Okay."

The following day, I went over to Sara's place, and when she opened the door, she held a framed photograph in her hand, a leftover that didn't sell in the days prior.

"I want you to have this." She handed it over to me. When I turned it around, *Nadija's Street* was looking at me, waiting to be united with its new owner. I came home and hung it on the office wall right away. It became my daily reminder that home was still there.

## ❦ 20 ❧

### 9/11

I was sitting at my desk at work when commotion ensued. Someone yelled from their office.

"Oh my god, oh my god. Unbelievable." The voice exuded terror and fear. All of my colleagues congregated in the hallway connecting several offices. It was a beautiful day, sunny and as clear as glass. It was 9/11/2001. Greg came out of the office and in his flamboyant way announced:

"Planes got hijacked and crashed into the Twin Towers in New York City. Oh, my god. This is crazy." People started to pace back and forth, like chickens with their heads cut off.

I went back to my desk, opened up the internet browser, and looked up the word *hijack*. I didn't know what the word meant. It was the first time I ever heard it.

*Unlawfully seize (an aircraft, ship, or vehicle) in transit and force it to go to a different destination or use it for one's own purposes.*

Seize an aircraft *and* smash into two buildings? It sounded like the plot of a bad movie. Someone said that the hijackers also rerouted a plane and attacked the Pentagon building in Washington DC.

Who would do this? And why?

We gathered in the hallway and speculated as to what could happen next. Was this the beginning of a war? Were they coming to Boston as well? People were starting to say the Prudential Center and Hancock building were the next potential targets, but as the news just reached all of us, we didn't have details about the attacks. We didn't know what to expect. Fear grew in everyone's face and none of us could concentrate on our work.

The news spread quickly, like wildfire. People feared the worst, and didn't know what to do next, where to go. This sudden panic reminded me of the war beginnings in Sarajevo when we hadn't had the slightest clue why things were unfolding the way they were, and what to anticipate next. Everything was happening so fast.

The president of Harvard University sent an email announcing he would shut down the University for the day, and ordered an early release for non-essential workers.

I came home and turned on the TV replaying the images of the planes hitting the twin towers; the buildings falling into rubble. For a second, I thought of someone deciding to viciously knock down a tower of LEGOS a child had carefully built up over time, only to be destroyed in seconds. But this was no game. It didn't seem real until the TV showed dozens of firefighters covered in soot, fighting the fire enveloping what used to be two beautiful, tall buildings. The death toll rose by the minute, as firefighters unearthed the bodies, dead and alive. Mostly dead.

A lot of the scenes I'd witnessed, whether it was 9/11 on TV or a massacre on the main street of Sarajevo, looked like scenes from an action or zombie movie. It took a while for the mind to process the images, especially for someone who had already lived through trauma.

Even though I had no visible reaction to the events, I was shaken inside, and having a difficult time processing the evil. I had trouble sleeping that night, trying to imagine what it was like for someone on those planes to face such close death, to realize the end was near. Did they pray? Did they hope for the best? Did they know that hijacking was happening? What went on in their minds?

And for people who were minding their own business in the buildings, perhaps having a meeting, or having a telephone conversation, or giving a presentation, how did they feel when they felt the plane's sudden impact on the buildings? What were they feeling and thinking as the buildings collapsed? I tried to put myself in their shoes, tossing and turning until sleep came at dawn.

I was a mess the following day. I went to work where the atmosphere was somber, people still recovering from the recent news.

I'd get a request from a customer to schedule a classroom, and I would respond to the effect that, "I was personally affected by yesterday's events."

Her reply came within minutes, saying, *I am so sorry for your loss.*

Later, I learned that being personally affected by an event meant that you had a personal loss, that someone in your close circle had died. Perhaps, unconsciously, in the absence of any healing from my own past, part of me was responding to witnessing destruction again. I started noticing more noises being added to the list of things that made me panic and flee. I began noticing my boss chewing loudly, even though a partition separated us. I would put on the radio, but the loud chewing prevailed. I'd go outside for a break, hoping he'd finished eating by the time I returned. But it turned out the was a slow eater and he'd take bites between emails, so it would take him forever to finish his meal.

Feeling unsettled about the world we lived in and about my own surroundings, I resolved to find a new job. By mid-October in 2001, I began a new career journey in a different part of Harvard.

IN THE MEANTIME, MY HOME LIFE WAS NO PICNIC. MY LIFE was being hijacked by constant fighting and name-calling. And empty apologies. Matteo often complained about chores. Specifically, he didn't appreciate that we ate out at restaurants almost every night. He expected me to cook often, if not every day, but I was so focused on school, I had no time for anything else. We often went to an Italian restaurant in East Boston, and I slowly put on weight, so he often added a snarky remark about my weight gain. He traveled often for work and would be gone for days. I felt a reprieve on those days; studying seemed easier, as I didn't have to look over my shoulder constantly, anticipating Matteo to storm into my office and begin yelling.

When he returned from one of his trips one time, I noticed his wedding ring was missing:

"What happened to your ring?" I was surprised he hadn't said a word about it.

"I've lost it."

"You've lost it? How did you lose it?"

"I don't know." He refused to look me in the eye. "Maybe in my hotel room."

"Did you look for it?"

"Yeah, I did. I couldn't find it."

"That's awfully strange." I refused to believe he was telling me the truth, but I had to let it go. The ring was gone, a symbolic piece of our relationship that was dissipating like little bubbles in the air.

The tension grew day by day, worsening after he was fired from his job. He came home one day to announce that he'd been let go. It didn't surprise me in the slightest; I saw it coming after all the stories he'd been telling me about his job performance. Trying to save his reputation, I had written a letter to his boss one time, vouching for Matteo. I had written how Matteo worked hard and how extremely devoted to his job he was. I didn't tell Matteo I was going to do it, and one day he came home with the letter in his hand.

"Thanks for trying," he said.

In retrospect, I imagined his boss having a good laugh reading my letter, sharing it with all of the executives on the floor, cackling about it over a beer on a Friday evening. If anything, the letter might have made things worse for Matteo.

Matteo applied for jobs everywhere, but he barely got any interviews. He eventually landed a consulting gig where he worked on various projects. He became more distant, if that was possible given the vast distance already between us, and he often locked himself in the bedroom. I'd knock on the door just to check in and say hello, but he wouldn't even acknowledge it. The tension grew stronger with every day, and mean words flew in the tense air of our so-called home.

One day was especially bad. It was so bad that the memory of it still vibrates vividly in my head.

It was a regular Saturday morning, and I had just made the strong Bosnian coffee in a *džezva* and we sat at the kitchen table like any other day. But that morning, I could feel the heaviness in the air. Matteo began to complain about something trivial, raising his voice. I tried not to listen; his words flew by me like deadly bullets as I tried to dodge them. He stood and came up to me. He began sticking his finger at me and poking my arm so hard, multiple times as if he was trying to push an unwanted object where it didn't belong. I started to feel pain in my arm. Then it became numb. The rest of my body was brewing like the hot water I'd made for coffee minutes earlier. Matteo sat back in his chair and kept complaining, provoking, yelling.

Like a hungry lion in a cage, with all my might, my strength turned into viciousness, my arm reached for the cup of coffee in front of me. That cup of coffee and my mind were in no way connected. Anger took over me. My body completely ignored my mind. My rage came to the surface. I took the cup and flipped the entire hot coffee onto Matteo.

Shell-shocked at first, Matteo stopped talking and then he jumped out of his chair and began to chase me. I stood up from my chair, like a sudden tornado, and headed toward the bathroom. I closed myself behind and realized for the first time there was no key in the bathroom lock. I put my foot at the bottom of the door to prevent Matteo from storming in. I'd learned that trick when I was a child and our parents chased us around the house until we stormed into the bathroom. The trick worked. But my parents never yelled and screamed for us to come out like Matteo did. My body began to shake. I was sure that if I came out he'd hurt me, so I stayed in the bathroom as long as possible.

Minutes or hours passed, I wasn't sure how long. Then the storm finally calmed down.

The incident should have been enough for us to separate and start divorce proceedings, but I didn't know how to get out of the nightmare.

The tension didn't subside over time. We'd get into fights and I'd start crying, "I hate you, I hate you! And I want a divorce."

"You want a divorce? You'll get zip-a-dee-doo-dah." He'd slide his pointer finger and a thumb over his lips to emphasize the zip-a-dee-doo-dah part.

"I don't care! I don't want anything from you. I hate you. I can't live like this anymore."

During calm times at home, when he apologized and we'd seemingly moved on from a fight, my mind would trick me and tell me things weren't so bad; they could be much worse. I often compared my marriage to the war, and surmise that my situation was normal. I thought of all the people in the Twin Towers and felt fortunate to still be alive.

I continued to live in delusions, and daydream about having children, even though Matteo had told me the second year of our marriage that the two of us having children together would be a bad idea. As a trauma survivor, I could no longer distinguish right from wrong, good from bad, beautiful from ugly. Instead, I held onto hope.

But little did I know, Matteo had another surprise in store for me.

## 21

# HIT THE ROAD, JACK

I didn't see it coming at all. It had been days, months since the big fight, and we grew further apart. Matteo spent all his time behind the locked doors of his bedroom. He gave no indication that he was cooking up a plan behind my back and I never suspected it.

He was awfully calm one evening when we went out for dinner. When his rage turned into a state of kindness and calmness, I should have suspected the worst was yet to come. We were sitting at the restaurant table when he suddenly pursed his lips and then smiled. He looked me in the eye like he was about to cry and proceeded to share his news.

"I want to let you know that I got a job offer in Kazakhstan."

"Kazakhstan? Wow." I had nothing else to offer. The news shocked me. Ever since Matteo had been fired from his last job, he'd struggled to find permanent work. He was consulting on and off, but he wanted to have a permanent job with benefits. The times he'd locked himself in his bedroom, I should have suspected he was up to something he didn't want me to know.

"Yes, I'm leaving in a week."

"A week? That soon?"

"Yes."

I had a lot of questions, but the only one I mustered was this one: "Where is Kazakhstan? I don't hear much about the country at all."

"It was part of the Soviet Union back in the day. It's been an independent country since 1991. I will be living in the capital Almaty."

I didn't know why—and I should have known better—but I expected Matteo to say I could join him after my graduation. I had about a year left of studying. But Matteo never said a word about me even visiting, never mind living there. I never asked.

What I did ask, since my life had been kicked into heightened survival mode again, was whether he could contribute to rent payments since I could not afford to pay it myself. I could not stand losing another home.

"Yes." He proclaimed. "I'll be sending you money on a monthly basis so you don't have to worry about rent."

A week later, Matteo and I were on our way to the Boston Logan Airport in his leased Toyota Runner, half filled with his luggage in the back. We said our goodbyes, giving each other a long hug. I finally got to experience the happy Matteo, in his old element, adventurous and ready to take on the new world.

I went back to the car, sat at the wheel, and began to weep. I feared the coming loneliness, despite the fact my life with Matteo had been nothing but turbulent. When I calmed down, I turned on the engine and headed home. When I arrived, I opened the door and a strange feeling came over me, as though the sun shone on me, even though the day was rainy and gray. I looked around the apartment and felt a great sense of calm, as I realized the culprit for the constant fighting had gone. A huge smile formed on my face and, for the first time in many years, peace and quiet felt good. I sat at my desk and looked up Kazakhstan. I learned it was the ninth biggest country in the world with the population of only ten million. The land in the images I found looked deserted and cold.

I walked around the apartment as though I had just moved

in, discovering it anew as my own space. I claimed Matteo's bedroom and grinned at the thought of sleeping in a more comfortable bed while watching TV before falling asleep. I opened up the bedroom closet and noticed all his suits lined up as if waiting for better days, and smelled the heavy stench of mothballs. Matteo had put them in the closet to help preserve all his fancy suits. Perhaps the distance between us, like the mothballs, could preserve our marriage. But the mothballs stunk to high heaven, and I quickly closed the door.

THE HOLIDAYS WERE THE WORST. THE YEAR MATTEO MOVED to Kazakhstan, I spent Christmas alone, at my desk. Nobody invited me to join their celebrations. I had consoled myself that, as someone with the Muslim background, I didn't need to celebrate. I didn't need to be with people. But loneliness and heaviness wore upon my psyche and I envied the families and their smiles, the decorated Christmas trees, the gifts and wrapping I'd seen in commercials. I wanted the holidays to disappear as fast as a snowflake melting on a palm. Instead of unwrapping gifts, I would devote my time to studying, occasionally turning to the window and watching the snow fall in front of happily lit houses filled with loving family members—something I could only dream of.

Perhaps it was time to go back to Bosnia and call it my home again. But nothing in the country had changed since I left; the status quo persisted. People were diving deeper into worry and despair. What prospects awaited me there? What kind of job would I land? A lot of people were still jobless; some could barely get by. People became homeless, some chose death by suicide to end their suffering and pain. My family and friends back home often said how lucky those of us were who'd left the country, before or after the war. We no longer had to live through the aftermath of the war, with images of destruction everywhere, neighbors divided and distant. Ridden with stress and worries, I pictured myself waking up with an asthma attack every morning, gasping for air. I saw myself in my parents' room, stuck in my own world of rage and anxiety. I resolved to stay in the United States even though I had challenges and struggles there. The struggles I faced were ones I'd chosen consciously. The ones in Bosnia, I had no say in. If I stayed, if I chose to battle my new war, perhaps there would be a repose of some kind.

## ✣ 22 ✣

# HEALING PATH DESTROYED

A few months before Matteo left for Kazakhstan, we attended Sara's wedding on a beautiful summer day, on a small island next to Martha's Vineyard, privately owned by the Forbes family. Matteo, Bob, and I carpooled together. We took a small, private boat from the mainland to the island. My recollection of her wedding is faint; my only remaining memories are of me clinging to Sara's best friend who was originally from Serbia, following him around and confiding in him like he was my best friend, too. I kept telling him how my marriage was unhappy, but he avoided me like the plague and kept disappearing.

Matteo got so drunk that, at the end of the night, he could barely walk and stand up. The three of us took the boat back to the mainland and had to search for our car for the longest time. On our way back, I drove and ended up taking the wrong turn, looping toward Cape Cod again, in the opposite direction to our destination. In his drunken state, Matteo finally realized when we were miles away and then began yelling about the missed exit, another opportunity to increase my anxiety and feelings of inadequacy.

Now that Sara was married, I saw her less often. I missed her.

She thought it would be a good idea for me to attend yoga classes in the studio where she'd recently gotten a job as a manager. With Matteo's departure, my world seemed to be widening. I was becoming open to new experiences. Sara told me that yoga was good for both body and soul, something I could benefit from right now, given all the stress I was experiencing. I was willing to try anything that could bring more peace into my life. I was searching for ways to combat loneliness, past trauma, and help my body relax. I felt tense all the time. My anxiety would come at the most importune moments in school, at work, and in social situations.

One day I was chatting with a colleague in a hallway. As we spoke, my mind became an empty black canvas and my head began to spin. My eyes rolled back in their sockets and it felt like my mind left my body for a second. It reminded me of the time when, at six-years old, I was under anesthesia and I dreamed I was falling between rocks into a huge hole, and I kept hearing a voice calling me to come back. The fall didn't end until I woke up in bed with my mother by my side. The feeling of a sudden loss of consciousness, as if someone had stolen my mind and left my body there to suffer, came upon me often. I'd try to be quiet in groups out of fear that these episodes—epic and embarrassing—would happen again. I'd put my head down and hold my hand to my forehead, trying to compose myself. That feeling of loss would last for God knows how long. It was my new reality. Perhaps yoga could help.

Sara sent me a contract to sign before my first class. The terms and conditions went something like this:

- *CLASSES WILL BE HELD FROM 6:30 P.M. TO 7:30 P.M. EVERY TUESDAY*
- *ALL PARTICIPANTS WILL ARRIVE IN CLASS EXACTLY ON TIME*

- *PARTICIPANTS MAY NOT BE ALLOWED IN
  CLASS WHEN LATE*
- *ALL PARTICIPANTS MAY BE SUBJECT TO
  DISMISSAL IF LATE PAYMENT TERMS
  SHALL BE COVERED PROMPTLY*
- *ANY FAILURE TO COVER PAYMENTS
  WOULD RESULT IN DISMISSAL FROM CLASS*

No big deal. All my life, I'd been punctual and never missed any payment.

The yoga studio was located between Davis and Porter Squares in Somerville. I'd come home from work, change my clothes and hop in my car to find my way to the studio. For my first class, I brought the signed contract for Sara to have on record and a check for the first payment. The classes weren't cheap, at least not for me, but I was slowly realizing that my well-being should take priority and I could take my health in my own hands.

I ENTERED A BUILDING THAT RESEMBLED A TWO-FAMILY HOUSE in the heart of Somerville and walked up the staircase, riddled with anxiety about this new experience. On the second floor, I slowly pushed open the door, as if a murderer were waiting on the other side. I entered the room where a few people had already placed their yoga mats and were waiting patiently for the class to begin. As I oriented myself, I noticed a big woman sitting at the very far of the room. She must have weighed at least four hundred pounds and was sitting in such a position that if you pushed her to one side, she'd fall and not be able to lift herself back up. She was our yoga instructor, Master Rose. *That was Master Rose? She must be brilliant at teaching yoga*, was my only thought.

At exactly 6:30 pm, our class began. Master Rose gave us

instructions, pose by pose, and eyed each one of us, correcting mistakes and missteps. Her loud voice carried through the room and we made sure to not repeat any earlier errors out of fear of the powerful Master Rose.

After the session, Sara came out of her office and greeted me. "So, what did you think?"

"For my first experience, I liked it. I think I'm feeling better already."

"Great. I'm so happy to hear that." Sara had her own dreams of becoming a yoga instructor someday and she thought that working with Master Rose would propel her to fulfill that dream. I showed up to the second session eagerly, already finding relief in yoga. I had not known that such alternative exercises could enhance peace and tranquility, a state I'd been craving ever since the brink of the war. Equally good, the second session brought me to peace and I began to look forward to the next class as soon as the previous one had ended.

Before the third session, I came home, put on a change of clothes and left the house at the usual time. Traffic to Somerville via Soldiers Field Road proved to be heavier than usual that day. I approached Harvard Square, and ran into a huge line of cars on JFK Street. Panic began to set in and I began to swear at the traffic, banging the wheel with my arm and screaming at the cars ahead of me. I hated being late. It reminded me of the days I walked through snow to my new middle school. If I was five minutes late, the teacher wouldn't let me attend class, so I'd have to wait for an entire forty minutes for the next class to begin. Traffic was out of my control. If I could have flown, I certainly would have. No such luck.

I parked at exactly 6:32 pm and ran to the building. I was huffing and puffing when I entered the studio, and there she was, in all her majesty, Master Rose, looking pissed.

"I'm sorry for being late." I announced.

"Have a seat." She maintained her sternness. "You are late."

"I realize. I hit heavy traffic on my way here."

"Did you read the contract?"

"Yes."

"What did the contract say?"

"What?" I couldn't believe she was interrogating me.

"I am asking what the contract said. Did you read it?"

"Of course. I read it and I signed it." I was getting more anxious by the second.

"So why are you late? You're making the whole class late. We cannot begin class until everyone is here. The contract is clear."

"Well, it was out of my control."

"So, what are you going to do next time?" I felt like years passed, not minutes, since her interrogation had begun. Everyone sat still like I was about to be executed, while a few others were fidgeting in their seats, seemingly anxious to begin their yoga routine.

"What will you do to prevent it next time?" She insisted.

I fell silent. I didn't know what to say. Suddenly, without planning to, I said, "I survived the war, I think I'm going to survive this, too."

A young woman sitting next to me let a loud laugh out.

"Quiet!" Master Rose's rage vibrated in the studio. "I hope this will be an isolated incident. I hope you understand that you disrupted the entire class due to your tardiness. We're now going to resume class."

I resolved never to return to Master Rose's class after that. Sara attempted to find a way to give me my money back, but I couldn't care less. Later, I learned that Master Rose was making Sara's life miserable by stalking her every move and listening in to her telephone conversations with clients. Perhaps Master Rose needed a kind of healing of her own. Whatever the case, Master Rose made a dent in *my* faith in the ability to heal. How she became a yoga teacher remains a mystery to me. But I knew I had to do something to confront the war demons that haunted my dreams, and recover from my bad marriage. I still wanted to find a way. There had to be a way.

## 23

# POST-TRAUMATIC STRESS
# DISORDER

While horrors of the war ended in November 1995, my internal war with my own memories of that terror continued. More than five years had passed at this point in my life, but the memories of people dying on the streets, of the suffering, the hunger and cold, of losing our most precious home, of our neighbors being killed, of realizing how evil humans could be to others, still haunted me.

At the time, I had no idea I was experiencing post-traumatic stress disorder (PTSD). In retrospect, it seemed quite evident. I'd shake each time I heard a car pass by on the street, thinking it was a shell flying overhead, and I experienced rage, depression, and anxiety every day. They'd each take their turn and grew within me like cancer. I didn't know what the cure might be; I was so stuck in the survival mode that it didn't occur to me there might even be a cure.

Once, Matteo's best friend reminded me of an incident of which I had no memory. It sounded as if he was talking about someone else, a person he might have accidentally encountered on a strange occasion. Apparently, we'd visited him in New York City when I first moved to the United States, and as we drove down the city streets I requested that we stop somewhere so I could buy a cup of coffee. Matteo said he'd stop as soon as he could. But I didn't seem too pleased with his answer. I began screaming: "I want coffee now! I want coffee now!" crying and banging my legs against the car floor. When the friend told me this story, I couldn't believe it was me. The fact I couldn't recall even a second of it told me I was in a blackout as the scene unfolded. It must have been frightening to witness such a scene. And now that I pictured it, I understood how an adult's tantrum could look terrifying to outside eyes.

The war demons were everywhere back home and within me. They took over our bodies and hung on, making our lives more miserable. I'd heard stories about people committing suicide after the war, because their drive to survive vanished when so little improved. PTSD went unacknowledged and untreated in the country; people suffered more than ever, trying to get by and function normally.

Anis had constant nightmares that made him scream and wake up in the middle of the night. Matteo introduced him to the video game Doom and the two of them would play on his laptop computer endlessly. The objective of the game was to kill as many beasts as possible to advance to the next level. As a player advanced, there were many twists and turns, with beasts hiding behind the wall or suddenly jumping out of nowhere only to attack and sometimes kill. I watched the game, but I had no interest in playing it. For Anis, this game had been a reality during the war. He'd been deployed to a number of battles around Sarajevo and the rest of the country, and he'd come back half alive, fear emanating from his eyes. My mom caught him wailing one night shortly after he returned from a battle on Mount Igman, and described the sound he projected as a siren or, yet worse, a beaten animal about to die.

Doom would usually provoke those nightmares, and Anis experienced them almost every night. He needed help. So did nearly the entire country. Eventually, he took his rage out on his family. He came home one day, walked into the kitchen, and broke every single dish in the cabinets. On other occasions, when Dženana started going to the kindergarten, he'd take her books and supplies and throw them out the window, leaving the child helpless and sad. Dženana would burst into tears at times, and he'd pull her hair and threaten to beat her. The marriage could no longer stand the daily trauma. Amra and Anis ended up getting divorced, as did many other people who married during or shortly after the war.

The problem persisted, but a solution was nowhere to be found. The war demons settled in every Bosnian home. I traveled far with them and tried my best to fight them, often unsuccessfully.

In my anthropology class, we studied the conflicts in Bosnia and Rwanda and my professor asked me to give our class a brief overview on Bosnia. I prepared a short presentation and on the day of the class, I sat at the end of the table, having a clear view of all the students eager to learn. I started off explaining the history of the former Yugoslavia, the diverse structure of population in Bosnia and then moved onto the subject of the war. But as my presentation advanced, I paused and found myself unable to utter a word. Like a tsunami, emotions hit me and I began to sob. In my attempt to hide my reaction, I stood up and stormed out of the classroom, finding a safe corner in the hallway where I shook in terror. My classmate, Eileen, a woman who'd traveled to Bosnia for humanitarian relief appeared before my teary eyes and began to console me. "Are you okay?"

After witnessing the war aftermath in Bosnia, she knew what I was feeling. She grabbed my hands, squeezed them tight as if to reassure me that I wasn't alone, and gave me a hug. I was hyperventilating. Deep down, I felt embarrassed about the whole scene that had just ensued, but Eileen was the voice of reason. She gently reminded me that my reaction was normal. When we went back to the classroom, the professor was in the middle of talking. The students pretended nothing had happened. After the class, they went back to their dorms, while I continued to face my ugly demons alone.

I didn't fear for my mental health until one day when I was all alone at home. I was watching TV, and my evening was like any other after work. I had recently discovered Jeopardy, and after my usual nap, I'd wake up, put the TV on, and watch the contestants spit out answers as Alex Trebek posed a question. But this particular evening when I woke up, I felt a bit uneasy. I felt an urge to harm my body, to do something so I would no longer exist. My body felt strange, as if parts of it had already died. I saw my soul flying around me, beckoning me to do the deed.

I wanted to end my life. But suddenly my mind regained control, and overpowered the evil, beckoning finger. I pushed those self-destructive feelings away, leaving only the fear at what had nearly happened. How I might have ended my life, I didn't know, since everything happened so fast. I had no time to think about it, to come up with a perfect plan. In the back of my mind, I imagined my family appearing like sweet little angels telling me to cut it out. I couldn't imagine the devastation in my mother's heart, had the force prevailed.

When I saw my friend, Bob, I told him what had happened. He was alarmed and told me to call him immediately if such a thing happened again. He repeated, "Call me, call me. Right away. You got that?"

I wish I'd sought help upon my arrival in the United States, but I came from a culture that didn't believe in therapy. We considered our friends and family members our therapists, as we poured our hearts out over a cup of coffee. A conversation between friends would be sufficient. If you sought a therapist, you'd be considered crazy. And my family, especially my father, had a distrust of therapists. When he was young, his younger brother fell ill after his brain was attacked by bacteria. It might have been meningitis or encephalitis, but I was too young to take note of this and understand, whatever it had been. I had never met the healthy uncle and couldn't picture him the way he'd been before. He was eighteen years old when illness took over his body. Up until then, he was the best student in class and my father would tell us with pride that his brother would read a book in one sitting. He was smart and he loved to read.

When the bacterium attacked his brain, he became dysfunctional. He could no longer speak well or enunciate his words. When a doctor saw him, they diagnosed him with schizophrenia and they locked him in a mental institution for most of his youth. My father always believed the doctors had misdiagnosed him and he never should have been locked up in a mental institution. After my uncle's death, my father cried, mourning the tragic life of my uncle Mustafa every time we mentioned him. As much as it pained me to see my father's eyes fill with tears, it was at these times his ocean-blue eyes were singularly beautiful. His eyes were the hue of blue that was striking against the red eyes and clear tears, like shallow Caribbean water. When Amra and I were younger, before we'd heard of dominant or recessive genes, we often complained—and insisted—that our parents explain how we ended up having our mom's brown eyes, not Father's blue ones.

Every time my father cried, I was reminded that he detested psychotherapists; they served no purpose if they could make the kind of misdiagnosis they inflicted upon Mustafa.

My uncle Mustafa, for as long as I had known him when he wasn't in the mental institution, spent his time in pajamas at my grandmother's, toothless, pale as a ghost, smoking cigarette after cigarette, his skeletal body growing thinner by the day. A bucket was placed next to his bed in case he had to throw up. As a child, I became wary of getting close to any bucket.

Ever since I was a baby, every Tuesday, my father dutifully slept overnight at my grandmother's place to help take care of his brother. As I got older, his absence seemed odder and I didn't understand why my father would abandon his wife and children. My mother didn't seem to like it; she was young and needed a daily companion. Over time, my mother grew a bit resentful of his habit. They often got into fights and screamed at each other about the smallest things, but there must have been a deeper reason that my mother never revealed, for her to be so triggered. She wanted to support her husband, but she also felt the children should be my father's priority.

When Amra and I grew a bit older, Dad's older sister would often call us, sounding as if she was reading from a piece of paper, reading random made-up garbage about both my mom and dad. When we answered the phone, she'd be in the middle of a sentence already, like she was rehearsing for a play that evening. We hung up, but she'd call us again and continue where she left off. We'd hang up again and report to Mom later that Aunt Bera had called. My aunt was single, never married. She was a published poet and famous among literates in the former Yugoslavia. She worked as a professor at the Sarajevo University and also spoke perfect French. Admired by men, she didn't let anyone close to her, staying single until her death.

Her habit of calling and harassing us seemed more comical than anything else to me as a kid. It wasn't so much an annoyance as it was another reason for my mom to resent my dad's family's misfortunes. My mother thought Bera had a few loose screws in her head, even though she was beautiful, educated, and caring toward her younger brother Mustafa.

As for Mustafa's fate, neither psychology nor psychotherapy were well-developed fields back in the 1970s. Still, I wish I had ignored the stigma about psychotherapy and had sourced support to encourage my healing process right away.

My marriage was counterproductive to healing. It was one thing to know that back home, during the war, my family and I were marked for death. Our neighbors wanted us exterminated. But it was another matter that my own husband further degraded my well-being by constant name-calling, and belittling, lacking any empathy for what I'd already endured.

Back in Bosnia during the war, the enemy wanted me dead. I

was the victim of aggression, of constant shelling and shooting that could have led to my death. Here, my husband wanted me to be different, better, perhaps even just gone. I couldn't, and I didn't, know how to fulfill either of those wishes. Dead or disappeared. Deep down, I didn't want to be either one. I have only my survival mode to thank for getting me through.

His family watched my displays of pain, one time as I cried because his Aunt Patricia forgot I didn't eat pork, and that was all she'd prepared for dinner. She apologized, but I felt hurt and bruised, thinking the cruelty in the world would never end. I didn't know if they thought of me as a brat or as someone who was deeply scarred and needed help. My feelings were upside down, like my life. I was tough and numb in my victimized state. I'd scream and fuss about trivial things, like a baby needing attention.

A lack of support can limit someone's faith in healing. If a person doesn't have support, they feel isolated, and believe they deserve the life they've been given. Ultimately, I gained the confidence I needed to feel better about myself and the world around me through education. To this day, I am grateful for the classes I took, the friends I met, and professors who inspired me. I can say for certain that education was an eye opener. It was my first and most important step to true healing.

## ₴ 24 ₴

# EDUCATED

My parents instilled the importance of education in us from an early age. My mother often said that Amra and I would end up scrubbing toilets if we didn't study hard. I didn't need her scare tactics since I was already a self-motivated, curious child who taught herself how to read and write at the age five. Surprisingly, even though my parents kept promulgating their ideas on the importance of education, neither of them ever took any time to read books to Amra or me. I was jealous of my American friends when they shared stories of their parents reading to them before sleep every night. Growing up, I'd had only a handful books sitting on a shelf among my few toys. We had a collection of stories by Hans Christian Andersen and a popular book *1000 zašto 1000 zato*, or *1000 why 1000 because* which was popular among children in the former Yugoslavia. The book literally asked one thousand questions and had one thousand answers to them. We also had a handful of other random children's books, but we rarely opened them.

At school, I excelled in every subject. I was often that kid in the first or second row, raising her hand to answer the question. I wanted to impress my teacher—a blonde, short woman, Suada

—who I looked up to and who always had generous words for her students. On one occasion, when she asked all the students to perform in front of the entire class as an extracurricular activity, my best friend at the time, Svjetlana, and I decided to sing a popular song named *Suada* and dance. We had no self-consciousness.

My schooling went astray when I moved to another school in the fifth grade, for the chance to study English instead of Russian. The decision devastated me, but in the long run, my parents convinced me it was worthwhile. My time in the new school didn't go as expected, as I didn't fit with the other children and they bullied me on a daily basis. My grades began to drop, and I slowly lost my self-esteem. Then eighth grade was disrupted by the war and one day, as though someone had turned off a switch, we stopped going to school.

I would have finished middle school and begun high school had the war not broken out. In the second year of the war, makeshift schools were made in the cold and moldy basements of residential buildings. Teachers would arrive on our doorsteps when we weren't under attack from the Serbs. The teachers brought single pieces of paper with lectures typed up and they'd tell us to learn from those. I graduated from high school in the spring of 1996, several months after the war ended.

ANN WAS THE FIRST PERSON I BEFRIENDED WHILE AT Harvard. We met in a fiction class run by a professor who was demanding and difficult. Ann was spunky and she often spoke up in class, arguing or counter-arguing points raised by other students. Her voice was raspy, but confident. She gesticulated while she spoke and I noticed her fingers wave like someone had made them from plastic and shaped them while still warm. I noticed that she resembled the stereotypical description of a witch, with hair like a broom and a pointy nose. If she'd worn a witch's hat, I'd have thought she was the real thing. I pushed those thoughts away until I learned one day, when we went out for drinks, that she lived in Salem, Massachusetts. Who knew? Maybe she was a witch?

She was married to a tall African man, and I didn't understand the whole deal with him. I gathered he came to the United States as a refugee with her help, but the future of their marriage seemed to be uncertain, even though she loved him deeply and wanted to stay with him.

She and I often went out for beers after class and Mark, her fellow student from another class, would accompany us. I enjoyed their company, but Ann's behavior was often questionable. One time, while casually talking to us, she did her best to hide the fact she was stealing the cute salt and pepper shakers sitting on the table. She grabbed her napkin and covered the shakers, then slowly dragged them across the table until they landed in her bag.

As I spent more time with Ann and Mark, it occurred to me one day that Mark was homosexual. He might have been the first homosexual I had become friends with, but that didn't bother me in the slightest. When I realized this might be the case, the next time I saw Ann, I told her:

"I think Mark is a gay." Ann burst out laughing. "Why is that funny? I don't mind that he is a gay."

When she composed herself, she explained to me that I shouldn't use articles to describe someone as gay.

"You say, Mark is *gay*. Not *a gay*." She let a loud laugh again.

Ann liked to boss me around. When we made plans to do stuff, she'd say "You do it," because she was either not feeling too well or she simply thought that my being younger meant I had more energy to expend on such tasks.

"You do it." She'd say, sharply.

"What do you want me to do, exactly?"

"Look up what movies are playing in the Harvard theater tonight. We can check out the Knight movie."

I called half an hour later and told her I couldn't find anything on the "Black *Night*" movie. I didn't know that a letter had separated me from finding the movie, and Ann later made sure to let me know that "she had a feeling I wouldn't know." We ended up going to see the musical Chicago since there was so much hype about it. For Ann and me, it turned out to be a huge mistake. Twenty minutes into the movie, we both began to fidget in our seats, occasionally looking at each other, shaking our heads, thinking the movie sucked. Her wavy fingers slapped my hand half an hour into the movie and she said, "Come on, let's go," quickly moving up the aisle and finding the exit door. Ann walked up to the ticket counter, bended over to look at the sales person behind the window, then demanded her money back.

"Sorry, but we don't do refunds according to our policy."

"What? That's ridiculous. I want my money back!"

"I am so sorry, but there's nothing I can do. That's just our policy."

Ann turned into a mad force I had never seen before, yelling at the sales person and demanding her money back. I felt her energy, and I was rooting for her, but the whole experience was uncomfortable. We walked away without the money.

I began to question whether my friendship with Ann was sustainable. My opinion of her further deteriorated when the professor asked everyone to share a story we might have written in our last class. Her story, which I thought was about her fake marriage, sounded shallow, lifeless, without any depth in character, and I wondered if she really thought it was good.

When my turn came, I read my story "Under Walnuts" about my maternal grandmother celebrating Eid after the war. I had written that story in a couple of hours, in one sitting, barely editing it later. When I finished reading the story, the professor looked at me and said, "You wrote that?"

"Yes, I wrote it."

"Wow. It is excellent. I am pleasantly surprised." That she

was surprised made sense, because she'd been giving me mediocre grades and didn't have much faith in my abilities as a writer
or short story analyzer.

Her words encouraged me to seek out a writing group at
Harvard and continue on my writing journey. It would be a good
opportunity to slowly distance myself from Ann, who I now saw
as a thief, a bossy witch, and a bad writer.

The world became my new playground, and I could choose
who I wanted to play with, who I wanted to call my friends.

THE DUDLEY HOUSE STOOD ALONG MASS AVE AT A STRANGE
angle relative to the other buildings in the Harvard Yard. I had
read somewhere that the writing workshop took place there
every week. The first week, I walked boldly into the room where
a number of people were already sitting in a circle having a
discussion. Feeling anxious about the first encounter, I blurted
out my name and announced I wanted to be part of the
workshop.

A friendly young man, with a slight British accent, greeted
me warmly and told me to join the circle and sit down. This
man, Phillip, who was pursuing a PhD in French literature at the
time, eventually became a good friend. We often got together to
talk about all sorts of things, but mainly about literature.

Phillip's adventurous side moved us beyond writing into art.
One day, he decided we'd make a movie. He wrote a script and
acquired a simple camera for us to film scenes. He recruited a
few of his other PhD friends and shortly after, we were on a
quest to make a film. He gave me the role of a Serbian woman,
Vera, who was supposed to have a heavy Eastern European
accent and be so emotionally disturbed that her relationship
with her partner was failing. How convenient.

It was a cold winter night when Phillip had me walk to a telephone pole in the middle of Central Square in Cambridge. Snow

was coming down with vengeance and my role had me picking up the telephone receiver, pretending to make a call, talking for a few minutes, slamming the receiver and walking away into the snowy night. After a few tries, my hands nearly froze and I tried to convince Phillip the scene was good enough.

When we had ample footage, we found an empty room in Dudley House and watched the tapes. Some of the scenes, to my surprise, seemed real and touching. It all played out well until, in one scene, Phillip and I were dancing in circles, facing each other, with our arms entangled and hopping and skipping like two lunatics. We stared at the screen and almost at the same time uttered, "Oh, my god. What daaaaa..."

We laughed in embarrassment and soon abandoned our movie project, renewing our focus on writing and putting together the next edition of the literary magazine, *The Dudley Review*. I learned that the committee decided to publish my story Under Walnuts, and I jumped up and down with happiness. I was that child again, vigilant in her craft, being published in the school magazine, *Elan*. My story got recognition, if only minor, and I began to feel confident, not only about my writing, but also about the world as a whole. Meeting new and interesting people opened up horizons and helped my recent experiences fade. I was expanding my circle of friends, and that circle would become precious and tight, bringing with it a feeling of home.

Belonging was no longer a foreign concept.

My experience of befriending good people was reflected in my good grades as well. I consistently got As and Bs, and I made it on the Dean's list a few times. My GPA hovered around 3.5 until I took Psychotherapy class and got a C+—my only C during the undergraduate studies—and that seemed to skew my whole GPA. But I was determined to keep going. As soon as I arrived home, I'd turn on my computer and start working on homework. My love for writing became evident when, after a number of literature classes, I finally settled on the literature and creative writing major. I wrote several papers a week and read nine to fifteen books per semester, absorbing every word like a sponge. At some point, I sounded like my professors while speaking, as if I was reading from a book, and words would come out of me freely, without fear of making a mistake as an ESL speaker. My mind became clearer and my tongue sharper, and I was no longer shy or afraid to speak up.

But not all my experiences afforded me this feeling.

I met Michelle in a Marine Biology class and soon learned that her cheerful personality expressed itself through her constant laughter. Her cheer seemed refreshing; her laughter reminded me of my mother's before the war. It was loud and healthy and it could be heard a distance away. But my mother's laugh was suppressed by the war and it never returned. It only occasionally rings in my memory.

I loved going out for a beer with Michelle after class. Two of our other classmates, Thomas and Brandon, would accompany us and we'd go to the bar in Harvard Square Rock Bottom. Our gatherings at Rock Bottom became frequent, as in every week, and on occasion, a teaching assistant for our Marine Biology class, Zack, would show up and join us.

We all sat at a table, drinking beers and laughing one time, when someone brought up dinosaurs and the ice age. Somehow, it surfaced that I didn't know the ice age resulted from an asteroid hitting the Earth, and Zack looked at me, with eyes wide, exclaiming, "What? You didn't know that an asteroid caused ice age? Are you serious right now?"

Michelle began to laugh. She took a sip of her beer and placed the glass on the table.

"Relax. You can't expect everyone to know that."

I could sense his annoyance. Perhaps I'd heard the cause of the ice age somewhere, sometime, but more often than not I had trouble relying on my memory. This was something trauma survivors often faced. I wanted to tell Zack my story about education in Bosnia and the fact that my entire high school passed in the war. Maybe he would have understood. Instead, I kept quiet and took a sip of my beer, clenching my teeth and trying not to cry. He wouldn't pay attention to me or look at me for the rest of the evening.

That's when it hit me, for the very first time, that education needed to be a vehicle for advancing ideas and the world, learning about oneself and others, and improving one's faculties. I concluded that being a good person outweighed the benefits of education. I could care less if a person had decorated his life with multiple fancy degrees if he treated people disrespectfully.

IN OUR NEXT CLASS, MICHELLE SAT NEXT TO ME AND SAID, "What are you doing next Wednesday?"

"Studying, probably. Why?"

"My blues professor just told us that BB King is going to be a guest speaker in our class."

"No way!" I didn't let her finish. She started to laugh.

"Can you believe it? The professor told us we could bring two people to class with us. Do you want to come?" The benefits of being at Harvard.

"Count me in." I couldn't wait for the unique experience of meeting a blues legend.

On the night, we gathered in Lowell Hall in the corner of Oxford and Kirkland Streets. A giant bus stood in front of the building, which I assumed was BB King's and his crew's. The amphitheater was already filled with people, and all the seats were occupied by the time we arrived. I sat on the floor in front of the chair where the legend would soon sit. A few minutes later, Michelle's professor came out and began lecturing on the subject of blues. He introduced BB King who then, in all his majesty, came out to a roomful of roaring applause. People were on their feet in disbelief that such a famous star was in such close proximity.

He spoke about his life, the way he was raised, and how he

developed his love for music and blues. I admired his sweetness
and humility; it almost seemed as if I was sitting across from an
old, good family friend and he'd tell me stories of his past that
my parents forgot to pass down to me. Toward the end of the
class, he played guitar and sang a song, and Lowell Hall seemed
to swell with happiness and surreal joy. At the end of the song,
he threw his guitar pick into the air, and I tracked it noticing it
land near my feet. When I realized nobody was reaching for it, I
propped myself up and grabbed the pick and stored it safely in
my small jeans pocket. He let us take pictures with him, and I
asked a person next to me to snap a couple of pictures of BB
King and me. In the pic, I have a huge smile and I am wearing
my glasses, slightly hugging BB King. He is looking at the
camera, his face covered in sweat, wearing a sweet, innocent
smile.

MANY PEOPLE I ENCOUNTERED AT HARVARD WERE DECENT
and good, and I made lifelong friendships with them. When I
joined the student association, I met Ivan who later became a
close friend. We often went hiking with our mutual friend Chris
to explore the beauties of New England, ending our days in a
local bar, sipping beers and reflecting on a wonderful day.

Another friend, Christian, once invited me to San Francisco
for a Thanksgiving family gathering one year, and I willingly said
yes. We also visited house parties all the time, and those parties
seemed more like the ones I frequented in Bosnia—we all felt
like one. As new people arrived in my life, and as the newfound
feelings of belonging lifted me, I knew I still had to face the
shadows of my past. I heard from Matteo occasionally, mainly
for logistical purposes. I'd go to the Prudential Center where he
had a post office box and open his mail for him to let him know
if he had received anything important. In the pile every month

was a rent check that I depended on, and it was my main motivation to travel downtown at least twice a month.

Now that the school was coming to an end and the graduation date was set for June 2003, I began to wonder what was next for me. I wanted to sustain the feeling of belonging, and perhaps it was time to consider building a family.

## ❧ 25 ❧

# GRADUATION

I stood at terminal E of the Boston Logan Airport and waited for the plane from Zurich to land. I checked the status and saw that the airplane had landed a while ago. I walked back to the glass door exit and stood there, fidgeting around, anxious to see my parents and Dženana walk through the door. This was the first time my parents had set foot on a plane or even traveled outside the former Yugoslavia. Later, my mother proudly related how they succeeded in ordering food on the plane and they knew how to order juice as opposed to coffee, without speaking a word of English.

Amra might have accompanied them had she not given birth to her second child earlier that year. The day she delivered the baby, I was in a meeting, sitting in a conference room of Holyoke Center. It was late January and deep snow covered the streets of Cambridge and Boston. Suddenly, my flip phone rang. I excused myself from the meeting and when I answered, I heard Amra crying on the other line. Were they tears of joy or pain? I didn't know, but I too began to weep.

"Hi" said an exhausted voice from the other side of the ocean. "It's a girl. A beautiful healthy girl." I began to sob from happiness. "We are going to name her Nadja." My sister announced.

Life for my parents then must have felt like a gift. They were one grandchild richer and their daughter was graduating, all in the same year. I was the first person in our nuclear family to graduate from college, and that was a big accomplishment that my parents were able to witness.

Matteo decided to come and watch me receive my diploma, too. He stayed with his brother in Framingham while my parents and Dženana occupied his old bedroom. On graduation day, the Harvard Yard filled with graduation gowns and if you looked at it from a bird's point of view, you'd notice a sea of black caps, like tiny little crows, concentrated in the middle of the yard.

We later moved to a diploma-awarding ceremony where the dean called out the names of all students and we came out on the stage to receive our diplomas. When he called my name, I walked out and saw, in the corner of my eye, my parents in the audience, clapping. Matteo was taking pictures. My mother's face seemed covered in tears, though I wasn't entirely sure in that moment. But when the ceremony was over, I saw those tears up close, and they were as real as the piece of paper I held in my hand, evidence I had graduated from Harvard. Summa cum laude. GPA: 3.46. Matteo took us to a steakhouse on Route 9 to celebrate. My parents, who had rarely dined in a restaurant, struggled with the dining etiquette. They didn't realize the napkin was to be placed on their knees, and they didn't know how to properly use the fork and knife to cut into their steak. When Matteo ordered oysters, they looked at me puzzled and turned to me like they'd seen a ghost.

"Šta je *ovo*?" What is *this*? my mother asked.

"It's a type of seafood. Try it." I encouraged her. My mother shook her head and made a face of disgust. Mom had a way of expressing herself, which was somewhat blunt and naïve at the same time. She'd been used to home cooking ever since she was a teenager, and she couldn't deviate from the tastes of stews and simple dishes, even during an important celebration.

When she ate the steak, she ate so fast that she emptied the plate within minutes. I had learned the same habit during the war—to clean up a plate quickly, as if someone was going to come out of a corner, extend their arm, and steal food from my plate. But as I watched her, I judged her, disapproving of her gestures and facial expressions, and wishing she'd be more open to new experiences like the rest of us.

After we ate our dinner, Matteo silenced the table and proceeded to give a speech. He found all the right words and said something about my incredible accomplishments and how everyone was proud of me. I leaned towards my parents and did my best to translate, like he was talking about someone else.

On his visit, I noticed there was even more distance between us, but there was a certain tranquil quality to it and I couldn't explain why. While I was busy taking my parents and Dženana to different parts of New England, he'd be doing his own thing, rarely offering to join us. I still held out hope that our marriage could improve. Now that my sister had had a second child, my biological clock was screaming at me, and I was daydreaming about having children of my own. Now that I had graduated, I was more ready to fulfill this step in my life. But an opportunity to talk about our future plans never presented itself during his visit. Matteo was wrapped up in his own world, busy taking care of logistics to make his life in a new country more permanent, until one day, he got on a plane back to Kazakhstan.

My confidence and sense of belonging grew like a wild mushroom in the middle of a forest. With all I had accomplished in the last several years, it hit me that I could shake the world and get myself out of rut and shackles by focusing on education. It propelled me to see the world from a different angle. It encouraged me to think about different points of view, different topics in life, and learn about myself. I was no longer interested in talking just about me and my war experiences and how they'd shaped me devastatingly. I was ready to move on and be a force for change in the world, a force for the better. Reflecting on what I had become and what I had accomplished, it became as clear as day to me: I was no ignorant stupid bitch, not by any stretch of the imagination. I now refuted those voices and shun them like death in disguise.

# THE BEGINNING OF THE END

I decided to further pursue my education and apply for a certificate in business and administration at Harvard Extension School. I had energy enough to keep going and I saw no prospects of moving to Kazakhstan or anywhere else for that matter. Meanwhile, Michelle introduced me to her friend Kelly, with whom she often went to the local bar, the Thirsty Scholar, in Cambridge. The day we met, Kelly offered me an Altoid by grabbing it from the box and putting it on a palm of her hand. I shook my head and told her I was a germaphobe. My response shocked her, and she did not appreciate my bluntness. Our friendship didn't start off on good footing. But when Michelle graduated in 2004, she moved to another state, leaving the two of us behind to bond.

On a visit to her mother's house in New Mexico, Michelle got invited to a New Year's Eve house party. She had been dating a music student at Berklee, a guy who was always broke and had no intention of making their relationship serious. At the New Year's Eve party, Michelle met the man of her dreams, who later inspired her to think about her life choices and her future. She arrived at the Thirsty Scholar one night, announcing that she'd fallen in love and she'd be moving to New Mexico to be with the guy she met at the party.

Kelly seemed skeptical, "How did you fall in love so easily? You just met the guy."

Michelle laughed in her usual way. "I just know. I can feel it. He's everything I always wanted." It would have been easier to believe this had she not had two marriages behind her already. Neither Kelly nor I wanted her to be hurt again.

"That's a bold move to make. But if you think it will work out, then why not?" I told her. I could compare it to my own experience, I knew what moving to a different state or a country meant.

Michelle was smart and she had unbelievable instincts. There was no topic Michelle couldn't discuss. Several weeks before she moved to New Mexico, we sat at the Thirsty Scholar, like any typical night, talking about relationships. She was on cloud nine after meeting her perfect guy. I began to tell her about my own marriage, details that I didn't divulge to many people. I told her how I was still hopeful that my marriage could perhaps turn around, as I had changed and become more mature in my dealings with Matteo.

Instead of validating my points, as I'd expected, Michelle offered, "I don't think your marriage will turn around. I'm sorry for the brutal honesty, but I don't think it will change. You've reached a dead end."

I turned silent and paused for a bit. "Really? You think so?"

"I know so." Michelle began to laugh, revealing her cheerful personality. "He has no intention of getting back together. If I were you, I'd ask for a divorce."

Michelle's words resonated with me for a while. They entered my mind signaling a welcome change in my life. I'd begun to observe my interactions with Matteo, or a lack thereof, and noticed how far apart we'd drifted, each in their own world.

Several weeks passed, and I mustered the courage to email Matteo and tell him I wanted to talk. I heard back from him immediately. We scheduled a long-distance phone call on a Saturday morning, before I headed to pick up my monthly rent check from the Prudential Center.

The phone rang, and my palms began to sweat. *How will he react when I tell him I want a divorce? Will he tell me I am a stupid ignorant bitch again? If he does, I take no part in it. I'll tell him kindly to stop calling me names, and I will no longer tolerate it.*

We began with niceties, the weather report, the declining economy in the United States. Then silence ensued. Then I spoke. "Matteo. I think we both know that this marriage will not work for either one of us. I have given it a lot of thought and I think we should file for a divorce."

"I agree."

I agree? I heard relief in his voice like I had just told him I'd bailed him out of prison.

"I think that's the best for both of us," he said. Silence again. "I wanted to tell you I have met someone here."

"Say that again?"

"I met someone here in Kazakhstan. We have been together for almost a year now. Her name is Nellie and she's twenty-three." She was two years younger than me. "I will call my lawyer Mike and we can start the paperwork process." It sounded as if he'd been preparing for this moment all along.

"Okay."

We hung up and my body felt like someone had just cut me in half. I didn't mind Matteo being in the arms of another woman, but I didn't expect this sudden news he had withheld from me for so long. He'd felt entitled to move on, while I had still held onto a sense of false hope, my daydreams. I felt betrayed, tricked, and mocked. He was the biggest scam of my life, and I wanted to get him out of it as fast as he'd come in.

Around the time I planned my divorce, my maternal grand-mother died. She was ninety-one years old and was ready to depart this world. I couldn't fly back home for her funeral, as I didn't have any money. For years after, I wondered if my grandmother came to my dreams in the most horrific scenes to express her anger that I was not present for her funeral. In my nightmares, her face looked different, her eyes were big and scary and I'd often find myself in her house where she died.

My mother fell into a deep depression. If war had stolen her infectious laughter, her mother's death stole all her smiles. Before my grandmother died, she'd uttered my mother's name and wanted her presence. She didn't want to depart before feeling her, touching her. Ever since, I'd catch my mother staring blankly while lying on a couch, her face etched with deep sadness. She seemed lifeless, disinterested in being around people. She seemed locked in her own world of pain and suffering.

Given all that was happening, I didn't prioritize my schoolwork. I was failing an accounting class. On one occasion, I overheard my classmate Karen, who was in my study group, complain about me to the professor and I heard my name repeated: Nadija, Nadija, Nadija. I eventually learned that the professor had failed me and I had to retake class in order to earn the needed credits.

I heard from Matteo's lawyer shortly after we decided to file for a divorce. I had no representation of my own, because I didn't have money, and I didn't know how to go about finding representation in the first place. I opened up the email and the attached documents and read something about our divorce being amicable. The documents mentioned irreconcilable differences. There was no provision to say how our assets would be split, how much money I would be entitled to, or anything like that. I took it that meant I was getting nothing from this divorce. But I as read through the pages, I felt indescribable relief.

Years later, when my mind had processed all the things that had happened in my marriage, I'd go back home and give my mother a hard time.

"Why did you let me get married? Why?" I blamed my

parents for my fate. If they could have prevented me from going to a place far away from home, why didn't they?

My mother, as always, teared up and tried to defend herself.

"It doesn't matter what I thought and wanted. You'd have done it no matter what I said or advised."

That in a way made sense. War had matured me beyond my age. My parents' influence had waned next to the teachings of the war.

When I first met Matteo, he often told me I'd want to regain all the time I had lost during the war. He said that those years had been taken away from me and while I could never get them back, I might consciously try to regain them.

Perhaps he was right.

⟡

THE DAY IN AUGUST 2004 WAS SERENE, AS IF I'D BEEN transported to heaven for a little while. I stepped inside the Cambridge courthouse where Mike, Matteo's lawyer represented him, and waited for our session to begin. The judge ordered us to stand up and to swear we would tell the truth. The whole process took less than ten minutes. Only ten minutes to be freed from the shackles of a bad marriage.

Outside the courthouse, Kelly was waiting for me; she'd taken the day off work to be my support system. The sun shone brightly and the world appeared beautiful and grand. As I emerged from the building, I breathed in the air, began to laugh, and saw the path to healing appear in front of my eyes.

Kelly approached me, gave me a big hug, and let out a healthy and loud laugh with me.

"Let's go get a drink and celebrate," she said.

"For real," I smiled.

The family life could wait.

# AFTERWORD

At the end of March, many moons ago, I celebrated my birthday with a group of friends at home. My friends were kind enough to pick a cake for me—chocolate, my favorite—and get the exact number of candles for my age. Thirty-six. We sat around in a circle and watched the candlelight on the top of the cake, flickering around from all the movement and commotion in the room. My friends sang happy birthday while I stared at the small flames, waiting to blow them out. When they stopped singing, someone shouted, "make a wish, make a wish!" Silence filled the room, anticipating this important moment.

What is a thirty-six-year old doing making a wish? Isn't that something for children whose wishes are still limited to candy, or a toy they saw in a commercial, those wishes being tangible and fulfillable? Isn't making wishes just a fun thing to do, perhaps an old wives tale of sorts?

Not long before my birthday, I had seen a shooting star and remembered that anyone who sees one should make a wish, and keep it to themselves so that it comes true. For my birthday, before I blew the candles, I paused, and with all my inner mental strength and capacity, I thought of the same wish I'd made when I saw the shooting star.

Despite superstition, I took my wish-making task seriously because, at that point in my life, I'd try anything.

My wish was this: I wanted to meet a man who'd become my life partner, and make a family with him. I knew that it wouldn't be fulfilled by simply thinking of it when seeing a shooting star or blowing candles on my birthday, but it was a chance I was willing to take. For many years thereafter, my wish got ever fainter as I got older and my biological clock whispered that my chance might be gone. The right man hadn't come along.

Many people have crossed my path. Those who didn't have a clue what I went through often rejected me, misunderstood me, pushed me aside, discarded me. Up until 2005, I had no idea I had post-traumatic stress disorder. When we experience traumatic events, such as war, where people are trying to kill us, we lose our faith in humanity and our trust in people. Our rage grows not only at the injustices of life, but ultimately, because we have no control over these horrific circumstances. In my case, I battled with depression and anxiety after the war, often being in denial, trying to pretend that everything was normal. But my depression and anxiety seemed to have been a people repellent, and I couldn't form meaningful relationships until I sought therapy.

In 2005, I started seeing a therapist who diagnosed me with PTSD. Perhaps I would have seen a therapist sooner had I not still been in survival mode, searching for a home where safety, love, and comfort prevailed. Without a doubt, I can see that therapy has its benefits. It helped me untangle the knot of my past. It led me to learn that what happened to me was not my fault. That I shouldn't hold onto shame.

I have also come across many people who were kind, and loving, and who believed and never lost faith in me. They taught me to forgive myself, to be open to adventures, to pick up new hobbies, to travel. I am forever grateful for their openness and empathy, for helping me feel human again.

Fast-forward to year 2021, we are in the midst of a global

coronavirus pandemic. For the first time ever, I have not seen my family in Bosnia for almost two years. Over the years, though, the bond with my mother has strengthened and I feel a deep and undeniable connection to her. I have finally come to accept her shortcomings, as well as my own. Acceptance is love.

We speak on a daily basis now ever since I discovered I became pregnant in early June of 2020. At my age, pregnancies are automatically considered high-risk—vulnerable and delicate. My mom would call or text me daily, ask how I was feeling, and offer tips for a healthy and comfortable pregnancy.

In December 2020, I gave birth to a beautiful baby boy. My wonderful husband, Chad, and I celebrate his three months, just a couple of days before I celebrate my forty-third birthday. I feel blessed that this beautiful human being is now part of my life. Just the same, I now understand and appreciate more the power of familial love, the unconditional kind my parents have always given me even when I felt disconnected, belligerent at times, wounded and lost. Ultimately, it is this love that carried me to the better side of life. Finally, it is time to put survival mode behind me and live a life.

Wishes do come true.

# THANK YOU!

I sincerely thank you for reading this book! If you enjoyed it at all, please leave a review even if it's only a sentence. I'm happy to answer any questions you may have, so do please get in touch with me by e-mail: nadija@post.harvard.edu